The Wright Brothers
They Gave Us Wings

This time, they carried the glider almost to the top of Big Kill Devil Hill.

"Ready?" asked Orville.

"Ready," replied Wilbur from his prone position.

Safely in the air, Wilbur warped the wings. There was an instant response and Wilbur glowed with joy. But as the glider curved, he became aware of a new instability. He adjusted the controls. There was little response. True, the glider turned. Still—although puzzled, he managed a safe landing.

On his fifth flight that day, Wilbur became aware of increasing instability. Then the left wing dipped far too deeply. Frantically he pushed the elevator control. He was too late. The tip of the left wing bit into the sand and he was hurled forward against the canvas elevator.

The birds all knew the secret of turning while in flight. But their secret was so deep no one could solve it. People said it was impossible for a heavier-than-air machine to fly. But Wilbur and Orville determined to show the world that it could be done!

ABOUT THE AUTHOR

Charles Ludwig, in addition to forty books, has written over one thousand stories, serials, and articles. These have appeared in nearly one hundred magazines.

As part of his research, Mr. Ludwig goes to the actual locations where his subjects lived and worked. He visited Kitty Hawk, Dayton, and the Smithsonian. He also interviewed Mrs. Ivonette Wright Miller—the only surviving Wright niece, who is in her 80s.

Mr. Ludwig says of *The Wright Brothers*, "As the book progresses, the drama increases. Kitty Hawk was a nightmare; Wilbur nearly drowned. After they had flown, they were not believed. Through it all, they worked on Christian principles."

ABOUT THE ARTIST

Barbara Morrow has illustrated many books for boys and girls. She enjoys working with a variety of styles of art and on various types of books. When she was growing up, she spent hours in the youth section of the book shop where her father operated a print and antiques gallery. She makes her home in Kent, Ohio.

The Wright Brothers

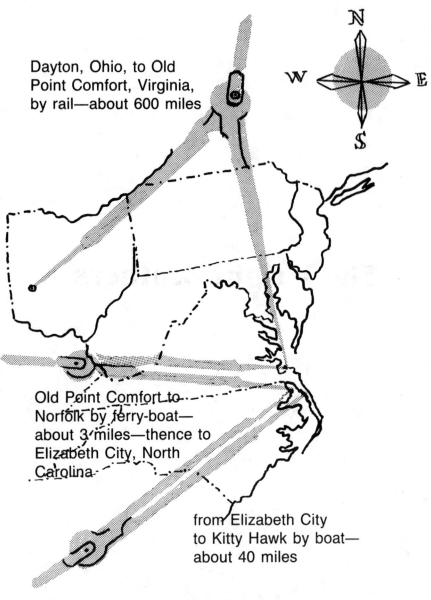

Dayton, Ohio, to Old
Point Comfort, Virginia,
by rail—about 600 miles

Old Point Comfort to
Norfolk by ferry-boat—
about 3 miles—thence to
Elizabeth City, North
Carolina

from Elizabeth City
to Kitty Hawk by boat—
about 40 miles

Kitty Hawk to Kill Devil Hill
by horse-cart

off Kill Devil Hill,
FIRST POWERED FLIGHT BY MAN—
120 feet

The Wright Brothers

They Gave Us Wings

by

Charles Ludwig

Illustrated by **Barbara Morrow**

MOTT MEDIA

Milford, Michigan 48042

Louise H. Rock, Editor
A. G. Smith, Cover Artist

LIBRARY OF CONGRESS CATALOGING IN PUBLICATION DATA

Ludwig, Charles
   The Wright Brothers: They Gave Us Wings

   (The Sowers)
   Bibliography: p. 179
   Includes index.

   SUMMARY: Recounts the story of the two bicycle makers from Dayton, Ohio, and their successful attempts to build a flying machine.
   1. Wright, Wilbur, 1867-1912—Juvenile literature. 2. Wright, Orville, 1871-1948—Juvenile literature. 3. Aeronautics—United States—Biography—Juvenile literature. [1. Wright, Wilbur, 1867-1912. 2. Wright, Orville, 1871-1948. 3. Aeronautics—Biography] I. Morrow, Barbara, ill, II. Title.

TL540.W7L83 1985   629.13′0092′2   [B] [920] 84-45447
ISBN 0-88062-141-9 Paperbound

For my son Charles Spurgeon Ludwig,
whose passion for model airplanes sent me to
Kitty Hawk; Dayton, Ohio—and finally
my typewriter.

CONTENTS

PREFACE

On Thursday evening, December 17, 1903, Bishop Milton Wright of the United Brethren Church sat alone in his upstairs study on Hawthorn Street in Dayton, Ohio. In spite of a pile of books on his neatly arranged desk, his mind was focused on Kitty Hawk, North Carolina. Numerous experimenters had been killed in their attempts to fly, and he was deeply concerned about the safety of his sons.

Kitty Hawk with its sandy hills and whistling winds was a treacherous place. For three years now his boys had been making trips down there in order to experiment with huge kites and gliders. This time they were equipped with a homemade motor and were actually going to try to fly in their heavier-than-air flying machine—something the wise ones agreed was impossible.

Letters from Wilbur and Orville had been alarming. One, although written in humorous style, had made him rub his beard:

> Part of the time we eat hot biscuits and eggs and part tomatoes. Just now we are out of gasoline and coffee. Therefore no hot drink or bread or crackers. The order sent off Tuesday has been delayed by the winds. Will is 'most starved.' But he kept crying when we were rolling in luxiuries, such as butter, bacon, corn bread and coffee. I think he will survive. It is now suppertime. I must scratch around and see what I can get together. We still have half a can of

condensed milk, which amounts to six or eight teaspoonfuls.

Another concerned the weather:

> In addition to 1, 2, 3, and 4 blanket nights, we now have 5 blanket nights, & 5 blankets & 2 quilts. Next comes 5 blankets, 2 quilts & fire; then 5, 2, fire & hot water jug. . . . Next comes the addition of sleeping without undressing, then shoes & hat & finally overcoats.

In order to push the grim reality from his mind, Bishop Wright tried to read a book. It was wasted effort. His mind returned to the boys and the machine they had constructed. At about 5:30 he began to smell supper. Moments later, there was a nervous rap at his door.

"Bishop Wright, I have a telegram for you," announced Carrie, the seventeen-year-old cook.

Methodically, Wright slit the envelope, read the message; and then in his characteristically calm way, handed it to Carrie. "Well, the boys have flown," he said. Later, he got out his tiny diary and wrote:

> In the afternoon about 5:30 we received the following telegram from Orville, dated Kitty Hawk, N.C. Dec. 17. "Bishop M. Wright: Success four flights Thursday morning all against twenty-one mile wind started from level with engine power alone average speed through the air thirty-one miles—longest 57 seconds. XXX Home Christmas. Orville Wright

As Bishop Wright studied the telegram, his daughter Kate breezed in. Eyes aglow, she exclaimed, "It says 'inform the press.' I'll take it to Lorin and he can deliver it to the *Journal*."

The clock in the newspaper office pointed to seven when Lorin stepped up to the night editor's desk.

"Fifty-seven seconds?" scowled Frank Tunison, interrupting him. "If it had been fifty-seven minutes we *might* have a story."

The Dayton *Journal* ignored the story. Other papers didn't. The *Virginian-Pilot's* headlines screamed:

FLYING MACHINE SOARS 3 MILES IN
TEETH OF HIGH WINDS OVER SAND HILLS
AND WAVES

Dismayed by such distortions, Orville and Wilbur refused to be interviewed. They even refused to show their pictures which proved they had flown. Their silence infuriated the press. Soon, reporters sneered that the brothers had never flown—that the story was a fabrication.

Tense years followed. Orville and Wilbur were largely ignored. Then on October 23, 1906, a Brazilian, Alberto Santos-Dumont, flew two hundred feet before cheering crowds in Bagatelle, France. The press now claimed that Santos-Dumont had invented the flying-machine! Moreover, they published photographs to prove it.

Although hurt, the brothers remained silent. Nevertheless, they continued to experiment, to make changes. During those years, their father remained confident. He knew his non-smoking, non-drinking sons were truthful. They had been raised on the Bible.

After a series of disappointments and incredible hardship, the Wrights succeeded in proving that they were the first ones to provide mankind with wings.

This book is the story of their struggles.

Inventors

All five of them, even seventeen-year-old Reuchlin—nicknamed Roosh—and his sixteen-year-old brother Lorin—were excited. This was because the kitchen calendar indicated the day had come for their father's return.

"I wonder what he'll bring us," said eleven-year-old Wilbur, his head cocked to one side.

Without answering, Orville, who was four years younger than Wilbur, opened the door and peered down the street. "He's coming!" he shouted. "Look! I can see him on his horse down the street!"

As the horse clip-clopped toward their home, Orville said, "I wonder if Father received my card." He had sent it all the way to Omaha. It was the very first postcard he had ever sent. Forcing himself to form each character just right, he had written:

Dear Father,
    I got your letter today. My teacher said I was a good boy today. We have 45 in our room. The other

day I took a machine can and filled it with water then
I put it on the stove I waited a little while and the
water came squirting out of the top about a foot. . . .
The old cat is dead.

Orville

There were disadvantages in being BKs—bishop's
kids; but there were also advantages. One advantage
was that whenever their father, Bishop Milton Wright,
returned from one of his numerous trips, he always
had a saddlebag full of gifts.

Within minutes Bishop Wright rode up to the front
lawn, dismounted, tethered his horse, and strode into
the house. ''You must be tired,'' greeted his wife,
Susan. ''I'll get you some cold water from the well.''

''Sounds great,'' said Wright. ''But first we must
water Jenny. Rode her thirty miles today and she's
tired.'' He sank into an overstuffed chair and rubbed
his closely-cropped beard. He stood up again. ''But
before we tend to the horse, I've a few things to show
you.'' He brought in his saddlebags and withdrew
some packages which he placed on the table.

As five pairs of eyes widened, he gingerly pulled
a mysterious object from a white box. ''Now watch,''
he said, as each eye followed his every move. Suddenly there was a blur. A bat-like contraption quickly
rose to the ceiling. It hovered there a bit and then
slowly descended to the floor.

''What is it?'' gasped almost everyone at once.

''Is it alive?'' demanded Wilbur, reaching for it.

''No. It's just made out of bamboo. Now watch as
I wind up the screws.'' (Later these were called
propellers.) When he released it again, it went to the
ceiling once more, hovered, and then slowly descended
to the floor.

''Let me wind it,'' said Wilbur.

''All right. But be careful. The power to turn the

screws comes from rubber bands, and if you twist
them too much they'll break.''

"Who invented it?" asked Orville.

"A semi-invalid Frenchman by the name of
Alphonse Pénaud.''

"Where does he live?" asked their mother.

"In France."

After Wilbur had released it, and it was settling,
he asked, ''Did the Frenchman make any that flew
on a level line instead of straight up?''

"He did. But I thought you'd like this kind better.''

Wilbur and Orville were so fascinated with the toy
helicopter, dubbed ''the bat,'' they didn't pay any
attention to the other gifts that were passed out. Three
days later, one of the rubber bands broke. Wilbur tied
it together, and it broke again. By the end of the week
the helicopter was a total wreck.

"Now we'll have to build another one," said
Wilbur. "But this time let's make it twice as big.''

"And where will we get the parts?" asked Orville.

"Oh, we won't have any trouble. We can get the
bamboo from the end of an old fishing pole, and I
know that Ma has some corks.''

"What about the rubber bands?" Orville looked
doubtful.

"We can buy them. We've already saved seventeen cents.''

Bishop Wright was generous. Whenever any of his
children wanted a few cents, they had merely to mention the amount, and his hand dipped into his pocket.
But Wilbur and Orville were too independent to ask
for money. Instead, they earned their own.

Cedar Rapids, Iowa, where the Wrights lived in
this year of 1878, had a fertilizer factory that
purchased old bones. Eyes open for business, Orville
and a friend dragged their wagons up and down alleys

and gathered old bones. As the pile in his backyard grew, Orville noticed a wide-hatted woman speaking to his mother.

"Those bones smell terrible," she said.

"Maybe they do," replied Susan Wright, "but Orville is a brilliant lad and he has a right to operate his own business."

"Well, if he were my son, I'd put a stop to it!"

"Yes, I know how you feel, Sister Snodgrass. But Orville is *my* son, and I'm proud of him."

Encouraged by what he'd heard, Orville worked harder than ever. Alas, the huge pile of bones brought a mere three cents. That, however, was not the only way to make money. Both Wilbur and Orville were dependable dish wipers. The pay? One cent!

Slowly Wilbur gathered the necessary materials to build the new helicopter. "Now it has to be exactly twice as large as the other." Ruler in hand, he measured each piece, and cut each one into the exact shape of the original. When heat was needed for the glue, or to soften and bend a piece of wood, their mother allowed them to use part of the stove.

After several days of work, and the purchase of a nickel's worth of rubber bands, the new helicopter was ready to assemble. "All we need to do now is to glue it together," said Wilbur. "Then, swoosh, it'll be up in the air."

"Can we fly it today?" asked Orville.

Wilbur shook his head. "Not today." As he spoke he sanded the screws, then twirled them to make certain they were properly balanced.

"Why not today?"

"Because the glue has to dry first."

"Maybe it would dry faster if you put it in the oven," suggested Orville.

Wilbur laughed. "No, that wouldn't work because

Ma needs the oven. And this type of glue is stronger if it dries in normal room temperature.''

As the contraption came together in the center of the kitchen table, their mother entered the room. ''Tonight we're going to have popcorn,'' she said, slanting her eyes at the enlarged helicopter. ''We'll be needing this table.''

''Yes, I know,'' said Wilbur. ''We'll have it all put away in an hour or so.''

''Fine. And since there's a lot of popcorn, we'll need some more firewood.''

''Don't worry, we'll bring in plenty,'' Wilbur assured her.

That evening as the family gathered around the table, Bishop Wright opened the new family Bible that he had bought in Omaha.

''This morning I put all your names and birthdays on the page in the front,'' said Bishop Wright. ''That will help us keep the family records straight.''

He opened the Bible to the family page and removed Orville's postcard. ''Thanks!'' he exclaimed, beaming at Orville across the table. ''It's now my bookmark. In time, historians may consider it valuable!'' This remark was followed by his own type of laughter. Although not a sound came from his mouth, his entire body rumbled like a house during a thunder storm.

Looking at the birthday entries, Bishop Wright said, ''I was born in a log cabin in Rush County, Indiana, on November 17, 1828. Those were hard days. Since we didn't have a stove, Ma cooked in the fireplace. Also, we didn't have the luxury of oil lamps like we do now. Instead, we had to use candles.

''My father, that's your grandfather, Dan Wright, worked in a distillery. But when he became a Christian, he gave that up and turned to farming. When

I was eighteen I also accepted Jesus Christ as my personal Savior. That was the greatest moment in my life!''

As the bishop was speaking, Susan Wright stirred the fire in the stove with a poker. Then she pushed in more firewood and poured some popcorn kernels into a large popper.

''I went to nearby Hartsville College,'' continued Bishop Wright. ''After I taught country schools for a few years, Hartsville College started a seminary and asked me to teach. That was a busy time! Besides teaching, I pastored a church. Then I met your mother. Her name was Susan Catherine Koerner, and she was the most beautiful woman I'd ever seen.''

''Come now, Milton. Don't exaggerate!'' exclaimed their mother.

''I'm not exaggerating. She was, and still is,'' insisted the Bishop firmly. He rumbled again and kissed her with such enthusiasm he twisted her pince-nez to an awkward angle.

''You shouldn't do that,'' she protested as she adjusted her small-lensed nose-glasses.

Bishop Wright went on. ''I went to Oregon as a missionary. That was in 1856—three years before Oregon became a part of the Union. At the time, I was twenty-eight. Soon I became the principal of a college. But my heart remained in Indiana. Distance and my letters persuaded your mother to finally say yes. I returned to Indiana and we were married on November 24, 1859. That was one week after my thirty-first birthday. We then—''

''You'd better pause,'' interrupted Mrs. Wright. She poured the popcorn into a large bowl and sprinkled it with melted butter.

''Before we eat, we should pray,'' said Bishop Wright, bowing his head.

As the family proceeded to toss the corn into their mouths, the Bishop continued. "After our marriage, we moved to New Salem, Indiana. There, I taught a subscription school and earned twenty-five dollars a month. Soon we moved to Fairmount, Indiana, and there Reuchlin was born on March 17, 1861."

"Those were happy days," said Mrs. Wright. "We had the luxury of a three-room log house, and a comfortable wood stove. I thought I was a queen, and was living in heaven."

"Less than a month after Reuchlin was born, the Confederates fired on Fort Sumter," added Milton Wright. He scooped up a handful of popcorn. "That attack plunged us into the Civil War." He shook his head and shuddered. "Those were dreadful, and yet exciting days. There were bands, parades, speeches. Lincoln was our president and three brothers of his wife died fighting for the Confederacy. I was often called to comfort a mother who had lost a son.

"Lorin, here, was born in the home of his grandparents in Fayette County, just east of Rush County where I was born. He came on November 18, 1862."

"And what great historical event followed his birth?" asked Reuchlin mischievously.

"General Burnside—he invented the breech-loading rifle and popularized burnside whiskers; today we call them sideburns—was defeated by General Lee at Fredericksburg about three weeks later. His defeat spread a blanket of gloom in the North. Thousands were killed.

"Wilbur was born on a farm near Millville, Indiana, eight miles east of New Castle."

"And what important event happened then?" asked Wilbur, as he rose to his feet.

"You were born on April 16, 1867," said Mrs. Wright. "That was the year Nebraska was admitted to the Union."

"If you don't mind, I'm going upstairs and look at our machine," said Wilbur. "I'm a bit worried about the glue."

"Aren't you going to listen to the rest of the story?" asked the bishop while reaching for more popcorn.

"No. I already know it. Orville was born in Dayton, Ohio, on August 19, 1871."

Orville continued, "And our sister Kate was born in the same house on the same day three years later. How could I forget it? Being born on the same day with her isn't fair."

"Why not?" asked Roosh.

"Because we only get one birthday party!"

As Wilbur led the way upstairs, Orville trailed behind. They'd just reached the top landing when their mother's voice stopped them. From the foot of the steps, she said, "In the same month and the same year in which Wilbur was born, Alphonse Pénaud, the one who invented your little bat, made a similar machine which he called a *Planaphore*. It flew over one hundred and thirty feet."

"Where did you learn that?"

"There was a pamphlet in the box the bat came in. I just read it."

"Did the Pla-Plan-aphore carry a man?"

"Oh, no. It was just the size of the bat and it was powered by rubber bands." She started to leave and then turned back. "One more thing. When little Kate was less than three months old, Washington Donaldson, along with two other men, decided to cross the Atlantic in a balloon named the *Daily Graphic*. His idea stirred the whole country. I read about it in the papers while I was feeding your sister."

"Did he make it?" asked Wilbur.

"No. He started in New York City and landed in the Catskills! They didn't have anything to guide the balloon, and so the winds pushed them in the wrong direction." She hesitated, and then added, "When you come down, I'll have some more popcorn."

Wilbur lit a candle from the flame in the lantern and held it close to the helicopter. "How does it look, Orv?" he asked.

After studying it closely, Orville replied, "It's ready to fly."

"Now let's go downstairs and get some popcorn." Halfway down, he stopped. "You know, Orv, I can hardly wait to fly it. We'll test her after breakfast. *Shooo! Zoom! Zip!* I already know how excited everyone will be. Ma and Pa's eyes will pop!" As if in a trance, he descended three or four additional steps. Then he stopped and faced Orville. "I've been wondering what I'll do with my life. Now, I know. I'm going to be an inventor!"

"What's that?" asked Orville.

"Someone who makes new things and discovers important secrets."

"And learns why clocks tick, and the sun shines, and why cans of water on a hot stove squirt?"

Orville's eyes widened.

"That's right."

"Then, that's what I'm going to be, too."

"And we'll work together. Right?"

"Right!"

"Then let's shake hands on our agreement."

Problems

Just as they began to hear sounds of pots and pans stirring in the kitchen, Wilbur and Orville rubbed the sleep from their eyes and scrambled out of bed.

"Is the glue dry?" managed Orville after a wide yawn.

Wilbur stretched, lifted the blind, and studied their new creation. "I—I—I think so," he ventured doubtfully.

"Then, let's make it fly."

"There isn't room up here; and besides I want the whole family to see its first flight. It will be an historic event!"

Orville frowned. "What do you mean?" He slipped into a shirt.

"This will be the first time such a big flying machine ever flew in Cedar Rapids." He yawned. "Now I'll attach rubber bands and see if the screws turn." He wound them until they were halfway tight. "Watch as I release them."

He released them. Neither turned.

"I know what the trouble is," said Orville. "The trouble is that the wood on the screws rubs against the wood on the helicopter. We need a slippery washer in between."

Wilbur bit his lip as he studied the helicopter. He held it toward the sun and viewed it from several angles. "I think you're right," he finally muttered. "But what can we use for washers?"

"I know! I know!" Orville exclaimed. "I've saved some worn-out buttons." He located one and held it up. "See, the four holes for the thread are broken and we can put the rubber band right through it."

"Do you have another?"

Orville did.

Moments later, buttons in place, Wilbur wound the screws. This time they turned, but not rapidly.

"Let's soap the place between the button and the wood," suggested Orville.

Soaped, each screw speeded at least three times faster.

"Now, when they're tightly wound, our machine will take off like a bird," said Wilbur confidently. "Just wait until—"

His sentence was interrupted by Kate. "Bweakfast's weady," she lisped. Opening her mouth, she pointed to a gap. "My tooth came out! Pa gave me a nickel."

Seven plates were at the table when Wilbur and Orville sat down. "We're having pancakes this morning," announced their mother.

"We'll now read from God's Word," said Bishop Wright, opening the family Bible. "I shall read Matthew 7:7-8."

Ask, and it shall be given you; seek, and ye shall find; knock and it shall be opened unto you: For every one that asketh receiveth; and he that seeketh findeth; and to him that knocketh it shall be opened.

After the Bishop had said grace, the family attacked their pancakes. While they were eating, Kate kept making marks on a slip of paper. "What are you doing?" asked Orville. He reached for the syrup.

"Am writing the number of pancakthe each one eats. Tho far, Pa hath eaten free and Lorin four. Ma hath—"

"And why are you doing that?" asked Wilbur.

"Becauth I like arithmetic. Ma ith helping me."

"When we get through, maybe you can tell us the average number each of us has eaten," suggested Lorin.

"I don't know how to do that," replied Kate. "I'm not in thkool yet."

At the end of breakfast, the family knelt around the table. Each said a prayer. Orville's included the petition, "And, dear Lord, may our flying-machine fly."

As the family seated themselves in the living room, Wilbur wound each screw. Then, as everyone watched, he tossed the apparatus into the air. But instead of rising to the ceiling, it merely wobbled and sank to the floor.

"Maybe we didn't wind the screws enough," suggested Orville.

Dismayed, Wilbur rewound the screws. This time they turned slightly faster. But again the machine dropped straight to the floor.

"It may be that you've wound them in the wrong direction," said their mother.

Wilbur frowned. "I don't think so," he said as he wound both blades in the opposite direction. "But we'll try it that way."

This time the helicopter dropped to the floor a trifle faster than before. "At least that additional speed shows that the screws are providing power," mused Wilbur thoughtfully.

Before the week had ended the brothers had tried every way they could imagine to make their bamboo machine fly. They added rubber bands, wound them tighter, tried it outside, and in the kitchen. Nothing worked.

Finally, Orville said, "Maybe it's too big, Will. Let's make it the same size as the one Pa gave us."

The smaller one flew just like the original. Then they made another big one. Again, it was a failure. As Wilbur and Orville were pondering this problem, their mother said, "The reason the big one doesn't fly is because God has a law that we don't understand. Your job is to learn and apply that law."

"What do you mean?" asked Wilbur and Orville almost as one voice.

"Our world operates according to God's laws," she replied. She removed her apron and sat down. "Some of His laws are easy to understand. Everyone knows that if we drop something it will fall straight down. This is the law of *gravity*. We also know that gravity makes water flow downhill. Some laws are easy to discover. Others are not. For example, think of the law of *specific gravity*.

"One day Hiero, the king of Syracuse, asked his jeweler to make him a crown out of pure gold that weighed a certain amount. In time, the crown was completed. But then he began to worry. *Is it pure gold, or did that rascal of a jeweler keep some of the gold for himself?* Determined to find the answer, he assigned the problem to a relative—Archimedes, the court scientist.

"Archimedes paced the floor as he agonized over the solution. Fortunately, when he was about to give up, he decided to relax in a tub at the city bathhouse. As he sank into the warm water, some of it overflowed. The overflowing water pointed his mind to an undiscovered law. That discovery so excited him, he leaped out of the tub. Forgetting to put on his clothes, he ran dripping and stark naked down the street while he shouted, '*Eureka! Eureka!* — I've found it!'

"The overflowing water had indicated to him that any bulk—his body for example—will displace an equal bulk of water. This means that since silver has more bulk per ounce than gold, it displaces more water than gold. Gold has a specific gravity of nineteen— that is, it is nineteen times as heavy as water. Today, that law is known as the *Principle of Archimedes.*"

Wilbur laughed. "This means that Orv and I have to discover why a helicopter that is twice as big as one that flies, won't fly. The thing that puzzles me is that a sparrow is much larger than a bumblebee, and yet it can fly even though its wings move slower."

"You are forgetting that a sparrow is a very strong bird. It consumes its weight in food every day. That would be like a sixty-pound boy eating sixty pounds of food each day. Also, a sparrow's heart beats from three hundred fifty to five hundred times a minute— that is, it beats five times as fast as the heart of a human being!"

Wilbur and Orville's eyes widened. "But, Ma, a bumblebee's wings beat much faster than those of a sparrow," said Wilbur.

"True. But a sparrow's wings are much larger than a bumblebee's. Also, if one wing is twice as long and twice as wide as another wing, it has four times the area."

"Four times?" Wilbur looked doubtful. "How do you know?"

"Through mathematics."

"Ugh!" Both brothers shuddered at the same time.

"Mathematics isn't hard. Bird wings are, of course, shaped in triangles. But let's assume that some strange bird had a wing two inches long and two inches wide. What would be the area of its wing?"

"Four square inches." Wilbur touched the tips of his fingers.

"Now assume that another equally strange bird has a wing that is four inches long and four inches wide. What would be the area of its wing?"

"Sixteen inches."

"And how much larger is sixteen inches than four inches?"

"Oh, Ma, don't rub it in. It would be four times as large," said Orville.

"That's right. Now if you boys are going to be inventors, you'll have to learn mathematics. It really isn't as hard as you think. Euclid is known as the 'Father of Geometry.' "

"His name, alone, gives me the shivers," said Wilbur.

"It shouldn't. One day this teacher of mathematics at the University of Alexandria in Egypt was asked to measure the height of the Great Pyramid. This was a tough assignment, for he lived about three centuries before Christ and didn't have access to our modern instruments. Also, that pyramid covers thirteen acres."

Orville leaned forward. "How did he do it?" he asked, wrinkling his nose.

"It was easy. He stood erect until his shadow became exactly the same length as his height. Then he said, 'Gentlemen, the Great Pyramid at this precise moment is exactly as tall as its shadow is long!' " She smiled. "What do you think of that?"

Orville shook his head. "I still dread mathematics."

"Nonsense! Any person can do anything. It's the *want to* that counts. Remember when you wanted to be promoted to the Third Reader?"

Orville grinned. "I remember. Teacher said that if any of us wanted to be promoted to the Third

Reader without waiting until the end of the year, we could go up front and prove to him that we could read the Third Reader.''

''And so what did you do?''

''I didn't have a Third Reader with me. But I had read it so often I knew the stories by heart; and so I went forward with my Second Reader and quoted a Third Reader Story.''

''And while he was quoting it,'' put in Wilbur, ''he held the Second Reader upside down!''

''But I was promoted just the same,'' concluded Orville after his mother and Wilbur had stopped laughing.

Both Wilbur and Orville had confidence in their mother's knowledge of mathematics and tools. Indeed, she seemed to know everything. Years before, in 1869, when their father was made editor of the denominational paper, the *Religious Telescope*, she often helped with his editorials. And when Reuchlin and Lorin had wanted a sled, she made them one that was just as good as those purchased in a store, and for one-third the price.

That afternoon Wilbur said, ''I really liked Ma's stories about Euclid and Archimedes. Let's repeat their experiments and see if they really work.''

''Don't you believe Ma?'' asked Orville.

''I do. But experimenting is fun.''

After a search in the stable, the brothers located a pile of rusty nuts and bolts. ''Now, let's go into the kitchen and weigh them,'' said Wilbur. Working together, they piled enough nuts and bolts on the scales to weigh a pound.

''We now need something lighter than iron,'' said the older brother.

''How about a piece of firewood?'' suggested Orville, placing a piece on the scales. The selected piece weighed a pound and a half. So they sawed off a third and kept trimming until it weighed exactly one pound.

Their mother appeared. "And so you're going to prove my story about Archimedes," she said. "Here's a basin you can substitute for his tub. But do it outside. We don't want water on the floor. And when you've found that he was right, don't go running down the street without any clothes on. Remember your pa is Bishop Milton Wright!" She held her arms akimbo and laughed.

Wilbur took the basin outside and placed it in a tub. Then he filled the basin to the brim with water. Satisfied that it was just right, he turned to his brother. "All right, Orv, put the nuts and bolts—I mean the crown—into the water and we'll measure the overflow." After pouring the spilled water into a measuring cup, he added, "Now we'll baptize our friend Archimedes by immersion as if he were a Baptist." He handed Orville the firewood. "Hold him under. But don't drown him."

As water flooded the tub, Orville scoffed, "I knew it would do that. Why did we have to prove it?"

"Because by proving it the fact becomes more clear." Wilbur shrugged. "Neither of us will ever forget the Principle of Archimedes."

To verify Euclid, the two persuaded Kate to accompany them to the Washington schoolyard where each was enrolled. When her shadow was four feet long, her exact height, they calculated the height of the main building and the tall tree near the entrance.

"I can hardly wait to tell Teacher what we've done," said Orville on their way home. "Her eyes will pop!"

About the time they reached their three-story home at 184 Iowa Avenue (now First Avenue), Kate asked,

"Why have you thtopped working on your flying-machine?"

"Because we've broken all our rubber bands and we're out of money," replied Wilbur.

"I have two nickelth, and another tooth ith looth," offered Kate.

"Thanks, but Pa said that we should earn our own way; and I agree," answered Wilbur. "By doing that, we'll own our own patents!"

While thinking about earning money, Orville had an idea. "Kids at school are chewing pine tar. Let's melt some and put syrup in it. It would taste great, and we could make a lot of money."

Kate smiled. "If it'th good, I'll wrap it with colored paper." She laughed and pushed out her tongue.

"We must experiment," said Wilbur. "Kate, you and Orv get the tar. I'll find a kettle and ask Ma for a jar of syrup."

Kate and Orville scraped handsful of the sticky pitch from several nearby trees. "Now, let'th take the dirt and bugth out," said Kate after she had turned on the garden faucet.

As the sap melted, Wilbur stirred in the syrup. Next, he spread a thick layer into the pan. After it cooled, he cut it into strips. "What'll we call it?" he asked, eyeing it triumphantly.

"Wright's Chewing Gum!" replied Orville promptly.

Eagerly, Kate thrust an entire section into her mouth.

"Is it good?" asked both brothers.

Kate tried to answer, but her mouth was glued shut like a trap. "Mmmm, mmmm," she went, as she tried to open her jaws. One hand on her forehead, and the other on her chin, she pushed, pulled, twisted. It was wasted effort. "Mmmm, mmmm, mmmm," she continued, as she tried one way and then another. "Mmmm, mmmm, mmmm, mmmm . . ."

"Let's pry her mouth open with a screwdriver," suggested Orville.

"Don't be silly! That would ruin her teeth!"

"She's losin' 'em anyway."

As they discussed the problem, Kate, utterly terrified, finally got her jaws apart. "It tatht awful!" she exclaimed. When she finally removed the lump from her mouth, she discovered that her loose tooth was sticking in the "gum." She made a face. "Ugh! Ugh!"

Wilbur laughed. "All things work together for good. Now Kate has earned another nickel! Trouble is, she took too big a bite."

After experimenting with their new product for a day or two, and rolling their eyes because of stomachaches, the brothers decided that Wright's

Chewing Gum was imperiled by too many problems—especially that of being forced to swallow castor oil.

Their next enterprise was the manufacture of stilts. And since they manufactured them out of scraps, there was little overhead. Their stilts were popular because they were assembled so that those who mastered them could turn them upside down, and thus be a foot or two taller.

The stilt business, however, came to a swift end. On a Tuesday evening after worship, Bishop Wright announced, "Next week we're moving to Richmond, Indiana. That means we must all start packing."

The children groaned.

"Why do we have to move?" ventured Wilbur.

"Grandma Koerner is eighty-four. She isn't well and your mother needs to be near her," he explained. Also, I've become the editor of the church paper, the *Richmond Star*. Richmond is a Quaker city. Each of you will acquire a lot of new friends."

"Will we be able to take our pet chickens?" inquired Orville.

Bishop Wright shook his head. "I'm afraid not."

"What will we do with them?" asked Kate, her eyes moist. "Clara Kluck ith thutch a pretty hen!"

"We'll eat some and give the others away," replied the new editor of the *Richmond Star* rather cold-bloodedly. He then dipped his hand into his pocket. "I forgot to pay you for your last tooth," he said, handing a nickel to Kate.

3

Businessmen

Wilbur and Orville found that Richmond, Indiana, was a better place than they had imagined. They had a barn, a brick house, and a spacious yard. Better yet, they acquired new friends. In the summer of 1883 the Barnum and Bailey Circus came to town. Viewing it as it paraded down the streets, Orville and his friends were goggle-eyed.

P. T. Barnum had just acquired Jumbo, a huge elephant, from the London Zoo. This elephant and the caged lions, tigers, bears, and other animals were an inspiring sight. The parade had hardly passed when Orville announced a new idea.

"Let's have a parade of our own," he said.

"Where would we get the animals?" asked Gansey Johnson.

"Easy," replied Orville. "Your father has a lot of stuffed animals. He even has a stuffed black bear and a stuffed grizzly bear. I'm sure he'll lend them to us."

"And what will we name our circus?" asked Harry Morrow. His voice was edged with excitement.

"It will be," replied Orville, "*the Great W. J. and M. Circus!*"

"What do those letters stand for?" asked Gansey.

"Wright, Johnson, and Morrow," replied Orville. He emphasized each name, and his tone was that of a judge.

In the succeeding weeks, the founders had daily meetings in which they discussed routes, admission price, and attractions. Wilbur was not a member of the company, but he agreed to arrange publicity.

Plans complete, Wilbur demonstrated his journalistic skills by writing the "press release." His copy bristled with such words as colossal, stupendous, rare, gigantic, and other superlatives. His account announced that the parade would be led by "iron horses," and that Davy Crockett would appear with a grizzly on a leash.

Heart thumping, Orville, along with some others, headed for the offices of Richmond's *Evening News*. With the release in hand, Orville noticed a box with a slot in it at the bottom of the steps leading to the editorial offices. Fearful of the ridicule he might receive if he were seen dropping an envelope in the box, he hestitated. But after he had worked up his courage by pacing back and forth a few times, he slipped it in and hurried home.

Hungry for news, and believing the story would interest readers, the editor composed an intriguing headline:

WHAT ARE THE BOYS UP TO?

Beneath this, he splashed Wilbur's story in full. He even included the price of admission: three cents for those under three, and five cents for all the others. He also added: "No adults will be admitted."

The article appeared in a prominent position in the September 10, 1883, issue.

On the appointed day, the parade lumbered down the street. The "iron horses" were two high-wheeled bicycles—one so ancient it had wooden spokes. Harry Morrow, although a member of the Board of Directors, was absent due to the fact that his parents insisted that he accompany them on a vacation in Michigan.

The main wagon had been assembled by placing boards lengthwise on an old buggy carriage. Instead of horses, eager volunteers, dressed as slaves, pulled the vehicle on which were "perched" a number of "rare" birds. Davy Crockett, his grizzly on a leash, was in the center of the wagon.

The Davy Crockett in the parade, however, was not the one who had trained for this coveted position. Corky Johnson, nine-year-old brother of Director Johnson, had forfeited this starring role by getting into an argument with the remaining directors. His place was taken by his brother, Griswold, who was not quite five. Because of this last minute transfer, there had not been time to arrange a new costume. This meant that Elder Johnson's boots and hunting togs almost swallowed him. Nonetheless, in spite of the fact that Corky shook his fist and vowed vengeance, Griswold was an enthusiastic Davy Crockett.

As the parade neared the center of town, Orville was terrified by the throngs that lined the street. "We'll never get them all into the barn," he groaned to Director Johnson.

"Then let's turn down an alley," suggested Gansey.

Tickets were sold at the door of the barn-turned-menagerie. But the crowd was so large only half of them could fit it. "Never mind," announced Orville, "there will be a second show."

Those who entered the dusty barn viewed a few rows of stuffed birds and animals. Each felt he had received his money's worth. Stumbling on a way to retaliate, Corky climbed to the top of the barn. Then, hands funneled to his mouth, he announced to the waiting guests that the second show had been cancelled. So there was no second show.

In spite of this misfortune, the Great W. J. & M. Circus was considered one of the most exciting events of the year. "That Bishop's Kid, Orville Wright, will really amount to something," was the opinion of many.

Shortly after this, Orville was captured by a new idea. "When we were small," he explained to Wilbur, "Grandpa Koerner told us that he hoped we could become woodworkers like himself."

The story the brothers remembered most about their grandfather happened to their parents right after their marriage. Milton and Susan Wright had just mounted the wagon which was moving them to New

Salem, when Susan exclaimed, "Oh, Milton, I don't have a rolling pin!"

"Never mind," replied a relative quickly. "I'll make you one in a moment." He fastened the discarded end of a beam into Grandfather Koerner's lathe. Minutes later, he presented the happy couple with a new rolling pin. It was still warm from its final sanding.

"Will," Orville said, "let's make a lathe."

Working together, the brothers selected some long pieces of sugar maple from the woodpile. Then they attacked the buggy frame they had used in the parade and selected parts they felt might be useful. As the parts were assembled, Orville had a suggestion. "Don't you think it ought to have ball bearings like the new safety bicycles?"

After thoughtfully scratching his head, Wilbur half muttered to himself, "To do that, we'll need some rings. And what will we do for ball bearings?"

"We can get the rings from that old horse bridle. Pa doesn't use it any more." Orville pointed to an old bridle hanging on a nail near a horse stall. "And we can use ordinary playing marbles for ball bearings."

"Mmmm. Will they be strong enough?" Wilbur asked with a frown.

"We can experiment."

The completed eight-foot lathe was powered like a sewing machine. The enormous treadle was long enough to accomodate six pairs of feet. When all was ready, several eager boys begged for the opportunity to pump.

As the lathe began to turn, there was a deafening roar. Wham! Swoosh! Shoooo! The boys assumed the noise was from the lathe. Then they began to smell moisture. Seconds later, a skylight flew off the top of the barn. Next, the entire barn began to shiver. Glancing out the window, Orville noticed that Kate was pasted to the door of their house like a paper target. As he shouted, "Cyclone!" he rushed outside and pulled Kate to safety in the cellar of their house.

The cyclone blew the roof from a church a mere two blocks away. But it didn't dampen Wilbur and Orville's enthusiasm for their lathe. Finding that their marble bearings didn't work, they replaced the bearings with a different kind. After several weeks of experimentation, their lathe began to earn money.

Then their father made a shattering announcement. "I have accepted the editorship of the *Christian Conservator*. This means we'll be returning to Dayton."

"To our home at 7 Hawthorn?" asked Orville, hopefully.

"Eventually. But since we've rented that place, we'll have to live in a house on Summit Street until the lease expires."

Orville beamed. "I can hardly wait until we get back to that Hawthorn house. I was born there, and I don't want ever to leave it. Ever!"

When Orville presented himself to the Dayton school system, he faced a problem. After examining his papers, the teacher said, "I'm afraid you'll have to repeat the sixth grade."

"Why?"

"Because you never finished the sixth grade in Richmond."

Orville's mouth went dry. "I—I—I completed the whole year except for the last two weeks."

"I'm sorry."

Orville's mind leaped back to Richmond. Two weeks before the end of the school year, he had gotten into so much mischief, his teacher, Miss Bond, told him that he could not return unless either his mother or father came with him and guaranteed his good behavior. But instead of doing this, he had merely stayed away.

"Why don't you let me try the seventh grade?" begged Orville.

The teacher hesitated.

"If I can't do the work, I'll be glad to go back to the sixth. Honest."

"Well, all right."

Orville applied himself. He often went to his mother for help—especially in mathematics. That year he made the highest grade in mathematics in Dayton and was duly promoted to the eighth grade. In spite of his grades, however, Miss Jennings, his English teacher, was certain she had seen mischief in his gray-blue eyes. Unwilling to take a chance, she said, "Orville Wright, move to the front row!"

By coincidence, Miss Jennings was later promoted to a position in the high school where she was assigned to teach algebra. Again she noticed those mischievous gray-blue eyes in her class; and again she said "Orville Wright, move to the front row!"

When Orville reported what had happened, everyone at the dinner table laughed, with the exception of the bishop. He merely smiled and rumbled.

Wilbur enrolled at Steele High School. His courses included mathematics, science, and history. Although he was not yet a member of the church, he had a feeling that he might enter the ministry. Schoolwork was hard for him. It was hard for him to keep his mind away from the athletic field. He had a passion for football and hockey.

Before leaving Richmond, Orville had become absorbed in the art of carving woodcuts. Now, living in Dayton, he discovered that Ed Sines was also interested in woodcuts and printing. Soon, he and his old friend formed a company, the purpose of which was to do job printing. Their first office was in Mrs. Sines' kitchen. When a letter came addressed to *Messrs. Sines and Wright*, she handed it to them with the dry comment, "I guess you are the messers!"

Pay for their printing often came in the form of popcorn and lollipops. This revenue caused a problem, for Ed felt it should be eaten, while Orville was convinced that it should be turned into cash. Since the partners could not agree, Orville bought his partner out for one dollar. From then on, Orville owned the business and Ed worked as an employee for wages.

Wilbur was employed by his father to fold and address the paper he published. Needing help, he hired his brother to do the folding. Orville soon tired of this. "All I do is fold, fold, fold," he complained. "Why can't we invent a machine to do the folding? It would be quicker and there would be less work."

Soon the brothers were searching through the barn. There they found pieces of wire, a foot treadle, rollers, and some other items they felt they could use. Then, heads together, they began to draw designs.

After lengthy arguments and a few experiments, the machine was ready. It was extremely noisy, but it worked.

Kites and Bikes

In addition to other ventures, the Wright brothers began to make—and sell—kites. As usual, they experimented with the features of their product. They wanted to build kites that would fly higher than those of anyone else. Also, they entered contests.

One Saturday, as their newest kite soared higher than any of their others, they discussed the reasons. "Perhaps it's because its tail isn't as long as the other tails. A tail can cause a lot of drag," suggested Orville.

"Let's find out," replied Will. He made a loop in the chord and then slowly wound it in. The boys tied on two more feet of tail and flew it again. This time it mounted just as high as it had done before.

"Maybe it's because it's lighter than the others," said Orville. "I made the cross frame as light as possible."

"It is lighter," agreed Wilbur. "But would an ounce or two make all that difference?"

Orville pulled it in a few yards and then let it out again. "Perhaps," he said thoughtfully, "it is flying higher because the frame is so light it bends in the air and puts a curve in the kite.''

Wilbur frowned. ''What would that have to do with it?'' he asked.

''I—I don't know. But, Will, the wings of all birds, even chickens, are curved. Also, it doesn't matter what kind they are—sparrows, robins, crows—they are all curved the same way. The curve is always at the front edge.''

''Maybe that's to give them strength.''

''Perhaps, and perhaps not. At a lake, I've sailed curved stones through the air to make them skim on the water, and they all seem to have a tendency to rise a bit.'' He tapped his teeth. ''Let's experiment. Let's make a kite that won't bend.''

That Saturday, the new unbending kite was in the air. It mounted quickly in the breeze, but it didn't go as high as the previous one. As they studied it, Wilbur commented, ''Maybe it doesn't fly as well as the other one because there isn't as much breeze as there was last week. Let's fly the other one and see what happens.''

''I can't. I've already sold it,'' confessed Orville.

Wilbur had other interests besides flying kites, continuing his schooling, and setting up businesses. After his conversion at thirteen, he had decided to become a minister. His plans included earning a degree at Yale.

He was also an excellent athlete. He played baseball, football, and hockey, and was one of the best gymnasts in the entire Dayton area. Being expert on ice skates, he soon became a member of the hockey team. When he was nineteen, as he was playing against a team of officers' sons from the nearby military installation on an artificial lake near Dayton's Soldiers' Home, an opponent lost control of his stick.

The heavy club smashed Wilbur in the mouth, split his lips, and knocked out most of his front upper and lower teeth. He received first aid from an army surgeon who happened to be present. Since his teeth could not be saved, he was eventually fitted with artificial teeth. But the psychological damage was even worse than that done to his mouth. He was convinced that his heart, already weakened by an early bout with typhoid, had been further damaged.

The accident ended his dreams of going to Yale. Indeed, it changed his whole life.

Now, a semi-invalid, Wilbur stayed home most of the time. Those around him were alarmed, for often he went into long silences and would only answer his best friends with monosyllables. Fortunately, however, he fell in love with his father's library. There, he spent many happy hours with Plutarch, scientific books, history, and even Greek. His reading also included the popular Goop books written by G. Burgess.

Susan Wright had become a victim of tuberculosis. Eventually she was confined to bed. Wilbur carried her up and down the steps each day. Reuchlin married in 1888 and moved to Kansas, then Lorin went away to a denominational college. At that time, Kate, now a young lady of fourteen, enrolled at another school—nearby Oberlin, made famous by the presidency of Charles G. Finney.

Much of the housework, including the cooking, was done by Wilbur. Sometimes he went to his mother and told her of his discouragement.

"It seems every door is closed," he repeated again and again.

"Nonsense!" his mother exclaimed. On each occasion she had a cheerful word. Once she said, "Wilbur, you have an inventive mind. I think you got it from my father. Someday you'll invent something that will help the entire world." On another occasion she commented, "Milton says that you're an excellent cook. He especially likes your gravy. Tell me, how do you make it?"

"Just as it should be made," replied Wilbur. A touch of pride laced his voice. "I always make certain the flour has been properly sifted. Then as I stir it in, I make certain that there are no lumps in it. I can't stand lumps!"

In the fall, a late postman delivered a letter from Reuchlin. "Read it to me," said Mrs. Wright eagerly.

As Wilbur read it, he came to the lines, "What does Will do? He ought to do something. Is he still a cook and chambermaid?"

Wilbur flushed. "I don't like that!" he said, tossing the letter onto the night stand. "When people don't have anything to do, they criticize me. Last Sunday I overheard a couple of women at church taking Orville and me apart. They said that we have a nice backyard and that we should make it into a garden." He scooped up the letter and handed it to his mother. "You'll have to read it yourself."

"Oh, Roosh didn't mean anything," she replied. "Jesus, Himself, prepared fish for His disciples. There's nothing wrong in being a cook. The Bible says, 'By their fruits ye shall know them,' and you've produced some mighty fine fruit. And there aren't many boys who could invent a folding machine."

"But people make fun of us," broke in Wilbur. "They say that we are too old to be flying kites, that flying kites is kid stuff."

"Let them talk! Ben Franklin was in his late forties when he flew the kite which proved that electricity and lightning are the same. Never mind the talk of small people! It takes courage to be different."

"I know that, Ma. Still, think of what I'm missing. Because of that accident I can't go to Yale."

"True, my lad. Nonetheless, you've learned to study on your own. You know your Plutarch and Archimedes. Being able to study on your own is *most* important. Lincoln only had a year and a half of formal schooling." She studied him for a long moment. Then she said, "Hand me my pinc-nez." After she had clipped the glasses on her nose, she pointed to a book on the dresser across the room. "Hand it to me," she said.

"You mean the book by Henry David Thoreau?"

"That's right. Thoreau was merely Emerson's handyman. Even so, he relayed some immortal ideas to the world. Listen:" She read:

If a man does not keep pace with his companions, perhaps it is because he hears a different drummer. Let him step to the music he hears, however measured or far away.

"Memorize that, Will. Let it become a part of your very being."

"I already have!" He stood up. "It's time to make supper. How about some nice brown gravy for the potatoes?"

Mrs. Wright smiled. "That will be fine."

Wilbur gradually began to mend. He continued to devour books; and, as a result of his mother's encouragement, his confidence slowly returned. Susan Wright, however, did not improve. Tuberculosis was all but incurable. Years in bed, sunlight, fresh air, and nourishing food were the general prescriptions in the 1880s. Wilbur supplied these. In addition, he read to her—especially from her Bible.

Mother Wright's favorite parts were such passages as, "I can do all things through Christ which strengtheneth me'' (Philippians 4:13), ''But my God shall supply all your need according to his riches in glory by Christ Jesus'' (4:19), and, ''For now we see through a glass darkly; but then face to face: now I know in part; but then shall I know even as also I am known'' (1 Corinthians 13:12).

When Orville was eighteen and Wilbur twenty-two they decided the time had come for them to found and publish their own newspaper.

''First of all, we'll have to build our own press,'' said Wilbur. Again they went hunting in the barn and woodpile. The needed roller was found at a junk shop. Since it wasn't heavy enough, they plugged one end with a wooden disk, filled it with sand, and then closed the other end.

The next major item needed was a heavy flat bed. Neither the barn, woodpile, or junk dealers had such an item. Then, as they were passing a cemetery, one of them had an idea. ''Let's use an old tombstone!''

As the apparatus was being assembled, many of the onlookers were convinced that it would never work. Moreover, they said so. But neither of the brothers would give up. Each time they faced a difficulty, they argued, made drawings, examined other presses, and kept experimenting.

When the new press was finally ready for a trial run, Kate joined the others who had appeared to see if it would work. As she studied the pulleys, treadle, rollers, cogs, flat bed, and wheels, Wilbur pumped the treadle. To the dismay of many, it worked. Even so, the brothers decided improvements were needed. In time, this product of the junkyard could print fifteen hundred sheets in one hour.

The *West Side News* went to press for the first time on March 1, 1889. Ed Sines had sold seventeen advertisements, and these were printed in good taste in the

four pages and three columns of the paper. Orville's
editorial explained the purpose of the new venture:

> This week we issue the first number of the West
> Side News, a paper to be published in the interests
> of the people and business institutions on the West
> Side.

The stories included one on the approaching
inauguration of newly-elected Benjamin Harrison,
who was a product of southern Ohio; an article about
Benjamin Franklin; and a leading feature about
Abraham Lincoln.

Bishop Wright studied that first issue with an
editorial eye, and was pleased to report that it contained no mistakes.

The first paper was distributed free. But within
weeks, there was a paid circulation of about four hundred. Sometimes the editorials were written by
Wilbur, at other times by Orville. Neighborhood boys
distributed the paper; and, when money was occasionally needed, the brothers borrowed small sums
from their mother. These debts were promptly repaid
on time.

Paul Dunbar, a slender black from Central High,
frequently visited the shop. He and the Wrights had
been friends from the time Wilbur and Orville had
launched the *Midget*—a school paper especially popular
at Central High. Once, when Orville needed a line
to fill a column, he mischievously wrote, "Deacon
Dunbar is in good health."

That line brought smiles to the faces of those who
attended classes with the blossoming poet.

One Saturday afternoon, Paul dropped in at the
office of the *West Side News*. Things had been going
well with Orville and he was in an expansive mood.

"Orv's just out of sight, eh, Deacon?" commented
Ed Sines.

Paul grinned. Then he ad-libbed, "Orville Wright is out of sight."

Liking the taste of that line, Paul secured a pencil and scribbled on the wall:

Orville Wright is out of sight
In the printing business.
You ne'er can find so bright a mind
As his'n is.

No one in the office at that time realized that those words would eventually appear in many books and that Paul Lawrence Dunbar would be known as one of America's great poets.

Since the weekly *West Side News* was doing well, Orville believed it should be expanded into a daily. With Wilbur as partner, a four-page, five-column, daily was launched. *The Evening Item* was well received.

But although it didn't lose money, neither did it earn any. After four months, the brothers dropped it.

Next, Wilbur and Orville agreed to publish *The Tattler*, a project promoted by their warm friend, Paul Dunbar.

While the brothers were experimenting with various enterprises, Susan Wright died on July 4, 1889. She was only 58. Later, Bishop Wright confided to a friend, "By his constant care, Wilbur extended her life by at least two years."

Both Orville and Wilbur had learned to ride high-wheeled bicycles while they were living in Richmond. Now, in 1892, a new European bike, dubbed the safety bicycle because both wheels were the same size, became popular. Unable to resist, Orville handed over $160 for one known as a Columbia. It was fully equipped with pneumatic tires. Also snared by the craze, Wilbur bought one. His was an Eagle. He bid on it in an auction for $80.

Soon Orville entered racing contests sponsored by the Y. M. C. A. Wheelman Club of Dayton. Although an excellent rider, Wilbur refused to race. Memories of his accident were still close to the surface. Instead of racing, he attended the contests in order to cheer for Orville.

As he raced, Orville remembered his mother's lesson on air resistance. "Notice the birds," she had said. "In a way, they are shaped like fish—small in front. None of them have abrupt edges. God made them that way so that they can slide through the air more easily."

While speeding by the sides of opponents, Orville would bend low and shape his body like a bird or a fish. With this advantage, he frequently won. He won medals for the half-mile, one-mile, and two-mile races.

After a race one day, Orville showed his father the medal he had just won. It was gold-plated, shaped like a silver dollar, and was suspended from a red, white, and blue ribbon. A large triangle with a "D" in the center was stamped on one side, and the words, 2 Mile Bicycle Race, on the other side.

Bishop Wright examined it closely. As he fingered it, his eyes moistened. Voice quivering from deep emotion, he said, "I'm mighty proud of you and Wilbur. Both of you have accepted Christ as your personal Savior. Neither of you drink, smoke, nor gamble. Both of you honor the Lord's Day." Then, resting a hand on Orville's shoulder, he added. "If you keep listening, the Lord will direct you—even though you have to cross the Red Sea!"

As the bicycle craze intensified, Orville and Wilbur gradually lost interest in printing. Instead, they sold bicycles. They opened a shop in 1892 at 1005 West Third Street in Dayton. Altogether, they handled eight brands: Fleetwing, Coventry-Cross, Reading, Envoy, Smalley, Warwick, Halladay-Temple, and Duchess. They also sold accessories.

The best bicycle brought $100.

The public believed in the brothers, and their business boomed. In 1893 they moved to a larger store at 1034 West Third, and listed their business as the *Wright Cycle Exchange*. As they sold bicycles, one of the brothers had a revolutionary idea. "Let's make 'em easier to ride by equipping them with balloon tires."

"But the fork isn't big enough."

"Then let's build wider forks!"

The balloon-tired bikes became popular; and even though business slowed in the winter, it expanded in the summer. Then on a momentous day in 1894, the brothers began to read the September issue of *McClure's Magazine*. That issue leaped into life with a feature story about Otto Lilienthal, a forty-six-year-old German engineer, who, from a high point, had managed to glide like a bird hundreds of times. One startling photo showed him whizzing through the air at an altitude of at least thirty feet.

As Wilbur studied the bat-like, double-winged machine with Lilienthal clinging to the lower bar across the inside of the bottom wing, he shook his head. "Look at that, Orv," he exclaimed. "Maybe we're entering a new age!"

The Wright Cycle Company

Eventually the Wrights needed something more challenging. Orville, bored by adding figures, invented a machine that could both add and subtract. Later they grew tired of selling bicycles manufactured by others. So they decided to manufacture their own. This was a daring move, for they had little money. Moreover, Dayton already had thirteen bicycle shops!

On April 17, 1896, *Snap Shots*, a Wright publication, announced:

> For a number of months, Wright Cycle Co. have [sic] been making preparations to manufacture bicycles. After more delay than we expected, we are at last ready to announce that we will have several samples out in a week or ten days, and will be ready to fill orders before the middle of next month. The *Wright Special* will contain nothing but high grade material.

The first Wright bicycle was named the *Van Cleve*. The name honored one of their relatives—Catherine

Van Cleve, an early Dayton settler. This bike was exceptionally strong. The tube-frame was brazed for added strength, and brush-coated five times with rubber-baked enamel. It had a new kind of hub-brake, and the buyer had a choice of handlebars. The buyer could also select the type of rims he prefered. Both wood and metal rims were available.

The first Van Cleve was sold to William A. Lincoln, truant officer and owner of a dry goods and clothing store. Bishop Wright helped close this deal by assuring the merchant that if he were not satisfied his money would be returned.

Lincoln enjoyed his bike and was often seen riding it on the streets while he rounded up absentees. Often, when it rained, he rode with an open parasol over his head. The machine lasted until 1919, at which time he gave it to the junk man.

The Wrights manufactured their own tools, including files, lathes, and wrenches. Strangely, although they wore aprons, they worked in white shirts, vests, and ties. Each was an expert at remaining spotless. When Ed Sines went to work for them, he, too, was required to wear a dress suit and tie.

As new tools were required, Wilbur and Orville invented them. The Van Cleve was followed by the *St. Clair*. This sturdy machine was named in honor of Major General Arthur St. Clair, a former officer in the Continental Army, and the first president of the Northwest Territory.

The St. Clair was cheaper than the Van Cleve. It had steel bearings, wire spokes, and weighed twenty-two pounds. Its narrow rubber tires were glued onto the wood or metal rims. As more business poured in, the brothers moved again. Their new location was 1127 West Third Street. (This is the building that was moved by Henry Ford to Greenfield Village in Dearborn, Michigan).

Neither Wilbur nor Orville could forget the article about Otto Lilienthal's gliding experiments. Each day they searched the papers for items about flying-machines; and often that was the discussion at the table. One day they came across some lines by Lilienthal that widened their eyes.

> During a gliding flight taken from a great height . . . I was unable—owing to fatigue—to draw the upper part of my body again toward the front. As I was then sailing at the height of about 65 feet with a velocity of about 35 miles per hour, the apparatus, overloaded in the rear, rose more and more, and finally shot . . . vertically upwards. I gripped tight hold, seeing nothing but the blue sky and little white clouds above me, and so awaited the moment when the apparatus would capsize backwards, possibly ending my sailing attempts forever. Suddenly, however, the apparatus stopped in its ascent, and going backward again in a downward direction, described a short circle and steered with the rear part again upwards and rushed with me vertically toward the earth from a height of about 65 feet. With my senses quite clear, my arms and my head forward, still holding the apparatus firmly with my hands, I fell toward the greensward; a shock, a crash, and I lay with the apparatus on the ground.

"What do you think that means?" asked Orville.

"I think it means that there are problems in the air that no one understands," replied Wilbur, shrugging his shoulders.

"But the birds understand them. Did you ever hear of a bird crashing? Maybe—maybe we should study birds."

Thoughts of flying dominated Wilbur's mind. One day a customer told him about a wilderness area beyond Dayton called the Pinnacles. "You ought to

go there,'' he suggested. ''There's a lot of wind around those peaks. It sort of blows upward. The birds have a great time soaring and swooping.''

With a pair of binoculars in his hands, Wilbur studied the birds. He noticed that they twisted their tails and also their wings. ''Maybe that's what we should do,'' he said to Orville, after describing what it was like.

While Wilbur and Orville wrestled with a way to twist wings, their friend, Cordy Ruse, was completing the first horseless carriage that ever sputtered down the streets of Dayton. The Wrights spent many happy hours with their friend as they discussed differentials and other seeming-impossibilities. In the midst of a discussion, Wilbur suddenly had an idea. ''I've thought of a great invention,'' he said. ''It's one that should be patented.''

''Tell us about it, quick,'' said Orville.

"My idea is to make a sheet that can be fastened under this new-fangled carriage that will catch all of the nuts and bolts that fall off!"

Ruse joined in the laughter. But he kept busy, and in 1896 the people of Dayton watched as he, perched high on the seat of his new carriage, proudly guided it down the street. Orville was so impressed, he said to Wilbur, "The horseless carriages will soon ruin the bicycle business. Maybe we had better start building them."

Wilbur laughed. "To try and build one that would run by any account you'd be tackling the impossible. It would be much easier to build a flying-machine!"

Orville studied his older brother closely. Then, arms akimbo, he said, "Will, that sounds great. But first we must learn the secret that will enable us to warp wings. As of now, that seems impossible."

During August, 1896, Orville was stricken by typhoid, an almost incurable disease at the time. While he tossed with high fever, and said wild things in delirium, Wilbur read some shocking news about their mutual hero, Otto Lilienthal.

The German engineer had continued his gliding experiments. On August 9th, he kicked off into a brisk wind from a hilltop in Rhinow, Germany. At first, his thin wings took him higher and higher. Then, as he neared the end of the flight, the glider nosed downward into the ground. Lilienthal's neck was broken. He died the next day in a Berlin clinic.

Comment about the accident was caustic. He was a fool, was the opinion of many. Even Lord Kelvin, famous for laying the Atlantic cable, did not believe that men would ever fly. He said, "I have not the smallest molecule of faith in aerial navigation other than ballooning."

Eventually Orville's fever broke. But Wilbur

delayed telling him about the accident. Remembering what the hockey stick had done to him, he feared
Lilienthal's death might end his brother's interest in
flying. As Orville's strength returned, however,
Wilbur spent many hours at his bedside discussing
the accident and the mistakes which had caused it.
"The wings of his glider were not wide or long
enough," he said.

"And he didn't know how to guide it," added
Orville.

Flying became the central focus of the Wright
brothers. They searched newspapers, magazines, and
the local library for information. The shortest
paragraph fascinated them. When friends sneered,
"You're wasting your time. If God had wanted us
to fly, he would have given us wings," they merely
smiled. Like Thoreau, both Wilbur and Orville had
tuned their ears to the beat of a distant drummer.

The 1890s were revolutionary. By 1899, almost
eight thousand cars chugged along the generally-dirt
roads of America. No Wright believed the automobile
would succeed. There were too many breakdowns.
Horses, trains, and streetcars were far more reliable.
Moreover, trains were making great progress. Huge
locomotives were blowing whistles and thundering
across America at unbelievable speeds. Some of them
occasionally peaked at sixty and seventy miles an hour.
Indeed, one could leave San Francisco early Monday
morning and be in New York City on Saturday noon.
Also, the Atlantic was being crossed by three-funnelled
steamers in six days.

Less than three centuries before, the Mayflower had
only averaged two miles an hour!

As the Nineteenth Century faded, and the Twen-
tieth approached, women were imprisoned in whale-
bone corsets, street-length skirts and high-buttoned

shoes. Also, more and more women colored their faces, using a crimson powder made of crushed insects technically known as cochineal, seventy thousand of which were required to make one pound of the reddish dye. Men, too, had their problems. Gentlemen were sentenced to wear stiff collars, cuffs, vests, and ties—even in hot weather. Though the times were grim, Wilbur and Orville were confident that they would fly. Their main problem was to understand the laws of God that would make flight possible. On May 30, 1899, Wilbur Wright made a significant move. He selected some paper and addressed an envelope to the Smithsonian Institute in Washington.

His letter read:

> I believe that simple flight at least is possible to man and that the experiments and investigations of a large number of independent workers will result in the accumulation of information and knowledge and skill which will finally lead to accomplished flight. . . . I am about to begin a systematic study of the subject in preparation for practical work to which I expect to devote what time I can spare from my regular business. I wish to obtain such papers as the Smithsonian Institution has published on this subject, and if possible a list of other works in print in the English language. . . . I do not know the terms on which you send out your publications but if you will inform me of the cost I will remit the price.

Fortunately, this letter was given to the assistant secretary of the Smithsonian—Richard Rathbun.

Although mailed on Tuesday, Rathbun managed to have a package addressed to Wilbur mailed on Friday, June 2. As Wilbur eagerly opened it, he found a list of books that he should read. This list included *Progress in Flying Machines* by Octave Chanute (1894); *Experiments in Aerodynamics* by Samuel P. Langley

(1891); and the *Aeronautical Annual* for 1895, 1896, 1897, edited by James Means (1895-1897).

Rathbun also included four pamphlets from the Smithsonian: *Empire of the Air* by Louis-Pierre Mouillard (No. 903); *The Problems of Flying and Practical Experiments in Soaring* by Otto Lilienthal (No. 938); *Story of Experiments in Mechanical Flight* by E. C. Huffaker (No. 1135).

Both Wilbur and Orville sat up late as they studied the books and pamphlets. Wilbur had expected the works to be encouraging. Instead, they were filled with histories of failures.

Hiram Maxim, inventor of the machine gun and brilliant engineer, had spent a fortune on a flying machine. He had failed.

Thomas Edison had invented the electric light, and the phonograph. But, although James Gordon Bennett backed him, the Wizard of Menlo Park concluded that flight was impossible unless a fifty horsepower motor could be developed that weighed less than forty pounds. The invisible word *impossible* seemed to be scrawled on every page of the pamphlets and the recommended books.

"What shall we do?" asked Orville.

"Read more books!" replied Wilbur.

Additional books were ordered, but like the others, they were all discouraging. Each implied: *the many difficulties are insurmountable*. Both Wilbur and Orville considered giving up. Why waste their time when their bicycle business was improving? Then each remembered the indomitable spirit of their mother— especially during the last month of her life. Her eyes remained fixed on the Lord. She had never said *impossible*.

The brothers had been raised on the Bible. They remembered Goliath and David's sling, Joseph,

Abraham, Moses, Paul, Deborah. These people had not given up. Nor would Wilbur and Orville!

The one light in their studies was Otto Lilienthal. He had never even attempted powered flight; nonetheless, he had survived over two thousand glides. True, he had been killed in a gliding accident. Still, his last words were a burning challenge. The stricken man had said,

"Opfer müssen gebracht werden!" (Sacrifices must be made!)

As BKs, Orville and Wilbur were well acquainted with sacrifice!

6

Kites, Balloons, Problems

Both Orville and Wilbur agreed that if they were to make progress in solving the problems of flying, they should acquire every fragment of knowledge available. Acquiring that knowledge meant that they needed time to read, experiment—and argue. Their growing business, however, meant that spare time was seldom available.

One solution was to streamline their work, to cut every unnecessary action. Their greatest time waster was glaringly apparent. Compressed air was not readily available. So, to save time, the Wrights kept a hand pump just inside the front door for customers who wanted to inflate their tires. Special wires were rigged so that when the front door opened an upstairs bell rang, and when it was closed a bell with a different tone was activated. Likewise, a wire was attached to the hook that supported the pump. Thus, when the pump was removed, the fact was registered on a secret meter. With this apparatus, the brothers knew when they had a potential customer. This saved brief moments for study.

Busy as they were, both Wilbur and Orville insisted on being immaculately dressed. Both ironed their own trousers. Each insisted that the creases be razor-sharp. And, in order that a flatiron would always be heated and ready, a few of them were permanently parked at the back of the stove near the chimney.

The history of kites was amazing. Invented in China approximately twenty-five hundred years ago, they had been used for signaling, propaganda, frightening evil spirits, measuring distance, pulling canoes from one island to another—and for amusement. One authority claimed that the only toy older than a kite was a doll.

During the Han dynasty, beginning about 202 B.C., a general decided to drive Emperor Liu Pang from the throne, which he had recently seized. The general was outmaneuvered. Fearing annihilation, the cornered general frantically searched his mind for a method to escape. Suddenly he had a brilliant idea.

In the dead of night he equipped a few kites with Aeolian strings and flew them over the enemy. Awakening out of his sleep, Liu Pang heard the wind blowing through the strings. To him, they seemed to be singing *Fu Han! Fu Han!* Feeling certain those words were a message from his guardian angel, he ordered his army to flee. The now triumphant general followed and cut them to pieces.

The brothers had published the story about how Ben Franklin had used a kite to prove that lightning and electricity are the same. Now they found another kite story connected to him. Orville read it out loud:

> I amused myself one day with flying a paper kite; and approaching the bank of a pond, which was near a mile broad, I tied the string to a stake, and the kite ascended. . . . I returned; and loosing from the stake the string, (I) went into the water, where I found that,

lying on my back and holding the [string] in my
hands, I was drawn along the surface of the water
in a very agreeable manner. . . . I have never since
that time practiced this . . . mode of swimming,
though I think it not impossible to cross in this manner from Dover to Calais.

Suddenly the bell clattered. And since the secret
pump meter didn't move, Wilbur zipped down the
steps. On his return, he remarked, "Sold another
bicycle tube. Now tell me more about kites."

"Lawrence Hargrave flew four kites together and
lifted himself sixteen feet into the air."

"When was that?"

"On November 12, 1894."

"Mmmm. That was only five years ago. Do you
have any other items?"

"Here's one about fishing with kites. It's done
mostly in the South Seas. A hook-line is attached to
the bottom of the kite. The writer thinks the kite
actually lures the fish!"

"There's no doubt about the power of the air,"
mused Wilbur as he paced back and forth. "Kites lift
men, pull canoes from one island to another, play
music, measure distances, carry packages. Surely,
Orv, there ought to be some way that men can fly.
California condors have a wingspread of as much as
eleven feet, and yet they soar without any trouble at
all."

"Maybe humans have been trying to fly the wrong
way," said Orville. "Sparrows and robins flap their
wings most of the time. But others, like hawks and
eagles stay aloft without flapping their wings at all.
Leonardo da Vinci designed a flapping-wing aircraft.
Maybe he was wrong."

Wilbur tapped his teeth and was thoughtfully silent

for a long time. After he had resumed his place at his desk, he said, "We've known about electricity for thousands of years. The word *electron* dates back centuries before the birth of Christ. It's Greek for amber. You see, the ancients discovered that if amber is rubbed with a cloth it will pick up tiny bits of matter. And yet it wasn't until recent times that we've known how to generate—and use—electricity. Edison didn't come up with the electric light until 1879. Let's see—"

He made a quick calculation with a pencil. "That was only twenty years ago!"

"True," agreed Orville, "and he was only enabled to develop that lamp because of a couple of preachers."

"What do you mean?" Wilbur asked.

"Edison knew that he had to pump out all the air in his light bulb. Otherwise, the oxygen in the bulb would burn out his slender carbon filament. Oxygen was discovered in 1774 by a preacher-scientist, Joseph Priestly."

"And who was the other preacher?"

"That was Michael Faraday—a lay preacher," answered Orville. "He made his discovery in 1831. Faraday discovered the principle of the electric generator. It was that discovery which made it possible for Edison to light his lamp. Electricity was in the world from the beginning. Noah saw lightning flash, and yet we didn't know how to make electric generators until sixty years ago! Experimenters were close, and yet—"

"The same is true of printing," said Wilbur. "The Romans were printing coins with words and pictures on them before New Testament times. Even so, no one thought of movable type until Gutenberg made his appearance in the middle of the fifteenth century." Wilbur shrugged. "His discovery was as simple as snapping one's fingers. All he did was to carve individual type that could be rearranged. A child could have thought of that!'' He became unusually thoughtful. While peering out the window, he muttered half to himself, ''Maybe it's that way with flying. Our problem is to think of the basic difficulties, and then overcome them.''

Orville closed the book he had been reading. ''Will, it's interesting to note how many of the discoveries that have changed the world have been made by deeply religious people. Isaac Newton spent years studying the Bible—and so did Copernicus. Copernicus had even studied for the priesthood!''

Wilbur laughed. ''Maybe I should have become a preacher! Ah, but the hockey stick ended that.'' He put his hand to his mouth.

''Maybe that was God's providence. Maybe God wants you to be an inventor!''

Their conversation was interrupted by the clatter of the bell.

After reading everything they could read about flying with heavier-than-air-machines, the Wright brothers concentrated on lighter-than-air-balloons.

''The story of balloons is facinating,'' said Wilbur one day after supper. ''The idea goes back to Roger Bacon (1214?-1294), and even before that. Bacon conceived the idea of filling a huge copper sphere with hot air and launching it from a high place.''

''Did he succeed?''

''No. He never tried it. Like a lot of us, Bacon had many ideas. But he seldom followed through. After him, a Jesuit priest, Francesco de Lana, came up with another idea for a man-carrying balloon. That was in—'' Wilbur shuffled through a stack of clippings. ''That was in 1670. He was a devout man. Gave up

his idea when it occurred to him that such an invention might be used for military purposes.

"According to this—" He pointed to a book on
balloons. "The first ones to make a balloon that lifted
a man were the Montgolfier brothers. Having
observed that smoke always moves upward, these
Frenchmen made a bag thirty-five feet in diameter.
Then, by heating the air inside with a charcoal brazier,
they managed to make it rise in the air.

"Three months later, in the presence of Louis XVI,
the brothers filled another bag. This bag was attached
to a basket in which they had placed a sheep, a rooster,
and a duck. When the air in the balloon was sufficiently hot, the apparatus ascended into the air. The
flight lasted eight minutes. King Louis was
overwhelmed.

" 'Now let's send a man up,' he suggested. 'And
since it is dangerous, I'll get you a criminal who's been
sentenced to death.' The Montgolfiers thought that
was a good idea. But the King's historian objected.
'Your Majesty,' he said, 'to be the first to fly would
be too much of an honor for a criminal.' This man,
Pilatre de Rozier, then climbed aboard and stayed
aloft for four and a half minutes."

"How high did he get?"

"Eighty-four feet."

As the brothers continued their research, they
learned that man-carrying balloons had been used by
Napoleon for military observation; and that the Union
Army had employed them during the Civil War. The
major problem was guidance. Moving higher or lower
in search of a wind blowing in the right direction was
impractical. "And guidance is *the* problem with
heavier-than-air machines," said Wilbur.

"If Lilienthal could have guided his gliders,"
agreed Orville, "he might not have been killed.

Guidance by shifting one's weight is not enough. Birds don't do it that way. We must study them.''

During warm-weather days, Orville and Wilbur made a practice of bicycling to Pinnacle Peak. There, lying on their backs by the hour, they studied the movements of birds. But even though they used binoculars, it was difficult to discover the exact manner in which the birds kept control of their flights. Sudden twisting of wings and tails was apparent. But the meaning of each twist, and the way it was accomplished was a mystery.

They were certain, however, that all birds could warp each wing independently of the other. While they puzzled, a flat package arrived from France. The return address indicated that it was from Captain Louis F. Ferber. The package contained an excellent photograph of seagulls in flight.

The brothers studied the photograph eagerly. It showed that gulls are experts at warping.

''The solution is that we must learn to warp the wings of any glider we may build,'' said one. *But how was this to be accomplished?*

Week after week each of the brothers drew diagrams of pulleys, cables, gears, and levers to do the warping. Each drawing produced heated arguments.

''That will never work!'' said Wilbur. He shook his head violently.

''Why not?'' demanded Orville, his eyes bulging.

''Because all those pulleys and gears weigh too much.''

Once when Wilbur had his arms outstretched, and was twisting each in a separate direction as he moved across the room, Kate stepped through the door. ''Have you started drinking?'' she asked as she stared. ''Or have you merely lost your mind?''

"We're just trying to find out how to warp the wings of a glider," explained Orville.

"Warp?"

"Yes, twist our wings in the manner of an eagle or buzzard."

Finding a simple method to warp wings seemed an impossibility. But the Wrights refused to surrender. They continued to order new books, make drawings—and argue. In the meantime, their business expanded. Late one evening, after a hard day at the shop, Orville was the first to retire. As usual, he left the gaslight burning for the benefit of Wilbur.

Orville was half asleep when he noticed that his now-asleep brother had failed to bolt the door. He got up, slipped the bolt in place; and then he had a peculiar urge to check the gaslight. Wilbur had developed a habit of blowing out the flame rather than turning off the gas. Having groped his way to the light, Orville was horrified that gas was still hissing through the outlet. Had he not turned it off, he and Wilbur would have died in their sleep.

"Your lives were saved by the hand of the Lord," commented Bishop Wright, as he attacked a slice of bacon. "I believe now, and I have always believed that God has His hands on you!"

Although discouraged, the brothers continued to draw diagrams of wings and cables and pulleys and gears—and to argue. Perhaps to compensate for his frustration, Orville raised a moustache. Then, in mid-July, 1899, at about 10 P. M., Wilbur found himself alone in the shop. As he worked, a customer entered.

"I need a tube for my bicycle," said the man.

Wilbur selected a long narrow box from the shelf and removed the tube.

"Is it puncture proof?"

"No, but it can be patched; and we have free air."

As the man considered the purchase, Wilbur unconsciously twisted the cardboard box one way and then another. Suddenly, as he was twisting, he noticed that he was *increasing* and then *decreasing* the length of the box. In a flash, he realized that he had discovered a simple method to warp wings. It could be done by twisting the *stanchions*—upright posts—that stood between the upper and lower wings of the glider he and his brother had visualized.

The customer paid for the tube and accepted the change. As he strode out the door into the warm air, he did not realize that he had just witnessed a discovery that would change the future history of mankind.

The Box Kite Test

As the new idea for warping wings bumped around in his head, Wilbur had to control himself to keep from running home. The idea was so simple. And yet! He felt like Archimedes after he had discovered the principle of specific gravity. All but leaping onto the porch of their Hawthorn Street home, he jerked the door open.

The living room gaslight was on. Otherwise, the house seemed empty. After glancing in the kitchen and upstairs, he shouted, "Orv! Orv!"

There was no answer.

Then he noticed a paper on the table. The penciled note in Orville's handwriting read, "Kate and Hattie have taken me to some kind of entertainment. There's pie in the icebox."

Kate had earned her degree at Oberlin in 1900 and returned home to live. One of her friends, Hattie Silliman, had been with them since Thursday. From the moment of her arrival, Kate had been taking her from one place to another. Reluctantly, Wilbur cut a generous wedge of apple pie, and seated himself across from the clock. Unlike Archimedes, he wasn't about to shout *Eureka*; nonetheless, he determined not to retire until Orville showed up.

He needed his younger brother's assurance and advice.

As he waited for Orville, he experimented with the paper box that had probably cost the manufacturer less than a penny. Eyes on its every move, he squeezed it in various places and then angled it back and forth.

The clock was in the midst of booming midnight when Orville and the girls showed up.

"Why aren't you in bed?" demanded Orville.

"Because I've found the secret of warping wings! Step over to the light and let me show you." As the girls disappeared into the kitchen, Wilbur demonstrated his idea. "You see, we'll warp them by twisting the stanchions at the end of each wing."

"Mmmm, maybe you have something." Orville spoke a little slowly. "Of course we'll have to make a—"

"Yes, yes, I've thought of that," broke in Wilbur eagerly. "First, I'll make a small model. Then I'll make a box kite and arrange it so that we can twist the stanchions while it's flying."

Orville and Wilbur worked together as a unit. They had a joint bank account, read the same books, attended the same church, enjoyed the same kind of food, and had the same projects. But on this occasion, Wilbur concentrated on the new idea while Orville took care of the business. After all, they needed a steady flow of cash while they experimented.

Wilbur fashioned the first model from split bamboo. The double wings were curved in the same manner in which Lilienthal had curved the wings of his gliders. In addition, they were flexible—especially toward the ends. He connected long threads to the stanchions, and, by pulling them, was able to warp the wings at a distance.

Yes, his idea worked!

Next, Wilbur built a kite on exactly the same lines. This one had a span of five feet. It was a foot across and was covered with cloth. Also, each wing section curved upward with the highest part of the curve near the center. Bird wings, he knew, were not curved in this fashion. Still, Otto Lilienthal was the master!

The finished, modified box kite, was ready on July 27, 1899. This was less than a week after he had conceived the idea of warping by twisting the stanchions.

While Orville remained at the shop, Wilbur took the new kite to an empty field just west of the city. He went alone. But as he arranged for the test, several schoolboys noticed him. To them, he was a curiosity; for it was indeed strange to see an adult man, dressed in fine clothes, together with a starched collar and tie, flying a kite. The boys followed him, then stood and watched.

Wilbur had arranged control lines attached to the stanchions at the end of the wings. These lines were attached to the four points of a wooden X which he held in his hand. By twisting the X he could warp the surfaces.

Soon the kite was high in the air. Now was the time to test his theory. Slowly he twisted the X and thus pulled one cord and relaxed the other. Yes, the kite was responding! He twisted the X in the opposite direction. Again, the kite responded. His heart fluttered with a new joy. He had solved a problem that had baffled giants! But just as he was congratulating himself, disaster struck.

All at once the kite swooped toward the earth. Like a hawk, it headed toward the boys. With no time to

run, the boys flung themselves to the ground face
downward and shielded their heads with their hands
and arms.

Down, down continued the kite. Wilbur's mouth
went dry as it headed toward the boys. Down, down
it continued. Then, at the last moment, he
remembered to twist the X. Seconds later, the kite
responded. It whooshed low over the boys and then
zoomed upwards.

Wilbur shook his head. But his heart raced. In his
mind's eye, he could see the glow that would come
to Orville's face as he related the story.

That evening, across the table, Wilbur told about
the events of the day. "We've solved the problem of
lateral control," he said. "Our next problem, Orv, is
that of *fore-and-aft stability*. I—"

He was interrupted by Kate. "What do you mean
by lateral control and fore-and-aft stability?" she
asked.

"By lateral control," replied Wilbur, "we mean
the control of the breadth of the wingspan, from the
tip of one wing to another. Fore-and-aft means from
the front of the apparatus to the rear."

"He means from the beak of the eagle to its tail,"
added Orville with a chuckle.

Now that Kate was back in Dayton to live, she was
hired to teach Latin and history in the Steele High
School. She suggested that a maid be employed to do
the housework. Carrie Kayler was only fourteen when
she accepted that position in February.

On the day she started to work for them, Orville
had a word of advice. "All of us like simple food. But
we're very particular about our gravy. It must be as
smooth as silk."

The next day's gravy was brown enough, yet it was
full of lumps. A few days later, Will found the new

maid stirring the skillet. After licking his lips, he said, "Now Carrie, let's pour this out and start all over." He then rolled up his sleeves, sifted the flour, and showed her how "good" gravy is made.

That year, Orville was twenty-nine. Teasing had become an obsession. His main victims were Kate and Carrie. "Carrie," he'd say, "you're so small you'll never amount to anything. Come over here and let me mark your height on the wall."

For months the gas lamp was just beyond Carrie's reach. Eventually, by standing tiptoe and stretching, she managed to turn it off. Excited, she rushed to Orville with the news. Orville responded by leading her to the measuring place. "Yes, you've grown half an inch," he affirmed. "That means that I will recommend that you remain with us."

Carrie not only remained, but she became almost a part of the family. She kept an eye on the brothers and was able to report to historians what their private lives were like. Wilbur, she remembered, was the most orderly. At noon he always entered the house through the back door, dropped his hat on a chair, combed his hair in front of the mirror, washed his hands at the sink, and took a cracker from a box on the sideboard. Next, he nibbled the cracker as he went to the front of the house.

Nibbling the cracker was the signal for Carrie to set the table.

After lunch, Wilbur always departed through the back door and headed down the alley. Moments later, he generally returned and picked up his forgotten hat.

Orville continued to tease, but he never forgot his hat.

In the evening, the brothers sat opposite one another in front of the fireplace and argued. As their voices grew loud, Carrie feared they were angry. She was mistaken. Arguing was one of their ways of learning. Frequently, especially if the argument was long, they changed sides.

Among the books Richard Rathburn of the Smithsonian had recommended, was the one by Octave Chanute, *Progress in Flying Machines*. Both Wilbur and Orville had read the book several times. Now they went after it as a dog goes after a bone. They analyzed each section and spent hours arguing over each conclusion.

Born to a distinguished family in Paris, Octave Chanute had migrated with his parents to the United States when he was seven. New surroundings provided opportunity to change his name. Originally, it was Chanut—a name close to the French words for naked cat—*chat nu*! Octave solved the problem by adding the *e*.

Chanute became a brilliant engineer. An expert on strains and stresses, he built the first bridge across the Missouri. After devoting himself to railroads, he spent his time studying flying machines.

As the Wright brothers studied Chanute's work, they decided that they would learn everything he knew. This meant that they would have to contact him personally. Because of his fame, this was an awesome thing to do. Nonetheless, Orville said, "He's as close as a postage stamp."

Wilbur agreed that he would write the letter. On a page of their stationary, Wilbur wrote:

May 13, 1900

Mr. Octave Chanute, Esq.
Chicago, Ill.

Dear Sir:
    For some years I have been afflicted with the belief that flight is possible to man. My disease has

increased in severity and I feel that it will soon cost
me an increased amount of money if not my life. . . .

My general ideas of the subject are similar to those
held by most practical experimenters. . . . The flight
of the buzzard . . . is a convincing demonstration
of the value of skill. . . .

Assuming then that Lilienthal was correct in his
ideas of the principles on which man should proceed,
I conceive that his failure was due chiefly to the
inadequacy of his method and his apparatus. As to
his method, the fact that in five years' time he spent
only about *five hours, altogether, in actual flight* is suffi-
cient to show that his method was inadequate . . .
Even Methuselah could never have become an expert
stenographer with one hour per year practice. . . .

My observation of the flight of buzzards leads me
to believe that they regain their lateral balance, when
partly overturned by a gust of wind, by a tortion of
the tips of the wings. If the rear edge of the right wing
is twisted upward and the left downward the bird
becomes an animated windmill and instantly begins
to turn, a line from its head to its tail being the axis.

After reading this letter, Orville said, "So you
believe that we need more practice in actually learning to fly?"

"Of course. Lilienthal was killed because he did
not know how to control his glider. Even an eagle
trains its young!"

Working together, the brothers decided that the best
way to attain practice in flying was to make a kite-
like glider, keep it permanently in the air in one place,
and learn how to manipulate it.

The only way a kite-glider could be secured to the
ground, and yet kept in the air, was to fly it in an
area where there is a constant wind of at least fifteen
miles an hour. In searching for such a place, the
Wrights wrote to Chanute and also to the U.S.

Weather Bureau. From these sources it was learned that the best probable place was Kitty Hawk, North Carolina. On August 3, 1900, Wilbur addressed a letter to the weather station there. Less than two weeks later, he received a reply from the station observer, Joseph J. Dresher. Wilbur read it out loud to Orville:

> In reply to yours of the 3rd, I will say the beach here is about one mile wide, clear of trees or high hills and extends for nearly sixty miles same direction. The wind blows mostly from the north and northeast September and October . . . I am sorry to say you could not rent a house here, so you will have to bring tents. You could obtain board.

Two days later, as Wilbur and Orville were discussing this answer, a letter arrived from William Tate, a former postmaster at Kitty Hawk. Tate wrote:

> Mr. J. J. Dosher of the Weather Bureau here has asked me to answer your letter. . . .
>
> In answering I would say that you would find here nearly any type of ground you could wish; you could, for instance, get a stretch of sandy land one mile by five with a bare hill in the center 80 feet high, not a tree or bush anywhere to break the evenness of the wind current. . . .
>
> You can reach here from Elizabeth City, N.C. (35 miles from here) by boat direct from Manteo 12 miles from here by mail boat every Mon., Wed. & Friday. We have Telegraph communications & daily mails. Climate healthy, you could find a place to pitch tents & get board; . . . would advise you to come any time from September 15 to October 15. Don't wait until November.
>
> If you decide to try your machine here & come I will take pleasure in doing all I can for your convenience & success & pleasure.

"I vote for Kitty Hawk," said Wilbur.

"I agree," replied Orville.

Their next problem was to build a suitable glider for their experiments. Since it was already the third week in August, and Tate had suggested that they be in Kitty Hawk by September 15th, they only had about two weeks to build the glider and pack it for shipping. Working feverishly just in back of their shop, the brothers assembled the necessary parts.

Each part had to be just the right size. The ash ribs for the wings had to be bent, bolts cut, holes drilled, hinges secured. Also, the smooth, white, French sateen cloth had to be carefully sewn so that it would fit snugly over the wings. In addition, slender cables and pulleys had to be arranged so that the wings could be warped.

"Why do you put a curve in the wings?" asked Kate.

"Because the curve provides airlift," explained Wilbur.

"Airlift?" She raised an eyebrow.

"Let me show you what airlift is," said Orville. He cut a thin strip of paper and held it in his hands. "Now look," he said. "The extended end of the paper is curving downward. Right?"

"Yes, of course."

"What will happen if I blow along the top surface?"

She shrugged. "That's easy. Your breath will bend it even farther downward. Even a goose would know that!"

"So? Let's experiment. But you hold the paper and you do the blowing."

While the strip of paper stretched out from her hands, Kate blew along its top surface. Instead of sinking, the strip moved upwards until it was almost straight. "That's amazing!" she exclaimed. "Why does it do that?"

"Because of the curve."

"But why?"

Orville shook his head. "No one really knows."

"Does the location of the curve or its height mean anything?"

"It does," put in Wilbur, as he took a piece of bent ash out of the vise. "But no one knows much about it. I believe the *camber*, that is curve, is extremely important. That word comes from the French verb *cambrer* which means to curve. A bird's wing is always curved at the front edge." He steamed another piece of ash so that he could bend it.

"According to the experts," added Orville, "we'll need two hundred square feet of wingspan to lift either of us. We've figured that out from the tables worked out by Lilienthal. You see, each of us weigh about 140 pounds and the winds at Kitty Hawk blow at about fifteen miles per hour."

Wilbur and Orville completed all the parts for the

glider with the exception of the eighteen foot spars which would form the front and rear edges of each wing. They had agreed that there was no point in buying these in Dayton and then transporting them to North Carolina when they could easily be purchased in Norfolk, Virginia.

As the days rushed by, it was decided that Wilbur would go to Kitty Hawk alone, and that if business dropped off, or if help could be secured, Orville would join him later.

On Thursday evening, September 6, 1900, Wilbur took his seat in a carriage of the "Big Four" and Chesapeake and Ohio Railway. His ticket was to Old Point Comfort, Virginia. As he tried to relax, he hoped he wouldn't have to endure tobacco smoke.

Within minutes, the big coal-burning engine was on its way. Did Wilbur Wright understand that he was starting out on a trip that would eventually threaten the entire American railway system? Certainly not! His one great hope was that he would discover at least one or two of the secrets that would enable the human race to fly.

Kitty Hawk

As the train gathered speed, the click-clack-click of the wheels beat a song of success in Wilbur's mind. Soon he was remembering how his mother had told him about the laws of God and how Euclid and Archimedes had discovered some of them. *Would he be as fortunate as Archimedes?* In the ecstasy of the moment there was only one answer: Of course!

Each daydream led to another. Soon his mother's favorite passage came beating into his brain. Strangely, the harmony of its words beat together with the rhythm of the wheels.

Ask, and it shall be given you; seek, and ye shall find; knock, and it shall be opened unto you (Matthew 7:7).

Yes, he had done those things. He had asked. He had sought. And now he was knocking. Likewise, his faith had wings.

Suddenly his flights into fantasy were ended by the stench of a cigar clenched in the teeth of an old man in the seat just ahead of him. Since there were several empty seats at the rear of the carriage, he promptly moved. About six o'clock the following evening, he dismounted at Old Point Comfort, Virginia. Here, he made certain that all his crates were safe and properly unloaded. Next, he transferred his things to the *Pennsylvania*, the steamer that ferried across a narrow strip of the Chesapeake Bay to Norfolk. After registering at Norfolk's Monticello Hotel, Wilbur had a quick supper and retired for the night.

In the morning as he ate his ham and eggs, he impatiently watched the slow hands of the hotel clock. While he waited for the time the lumberyards would open, he studied the map he had drawn of his final part of the journey.

"May I help you?" asked an old man who had stepped over to his table.

"Am on my way to Kitty Hawk, North Carolina," explained Wilbur.

"Kitty Hawk?" The man repeated the name slowly. "That's a strange name. Never heard of it."

Wilbur pointed to a long sliver of land that shielded the east coast of North Carolina. "It's right here," he said, pointing to a place about a third of the way down. "Am going from here to Elizabeth City, North Carolina. From there I'll hire a boat."

"Mmmm," muttered the man. "That's one of the most dangerous areas in America." He placed his finger on the south part of the sliver where the string-like land turns sharply to the west. "That's the Cape Hatteras Lighthouse. Tallest lighthouse in America. It was built to guard what's known as the Graveyard of the Atlantic."

"Why such a name?"

"Well, as a retired skipper, I can give you the details. The Gulf Stream flows north around there at a speed of three-and-a-half knots. That means that if a ship is going south at seven knots, its speed is cut in half. To go faster, some captains sail too close to the breakers. That's dangerous, for a little wind can blow them into the rocks. Since the 1500s, almost two thousand ships have gone down in that area. That old lighthouse—first one was built in 1798—has saved many lives.'' He studied Wilbur for an intense moment. ''But why would you, dressed fit to kill, want to go to such an obscure place?''

''I need a steady wind.''

''A steady wind?'' He frowned and twisted his head.

''Yes, to fly a glider.''

The puzzled look on the man's face deepened. As the man turned to leave, Wilbur stopped him with a question. ''Could you, sir, direct me to a lumberyard?''

The man drew a sketch and pointed.

At the lumberyard, after a long search, the clerk said, ''We hain't got no pieces of spruce eighteen feet long. But we've lots of pieces sixteen feet long.''

Wilbur visited many lumberyards. It was wasted effort. Finally, he selected four pieces each sixteen feet long. The shorter length meant that he would have to alter the sateen he had so carefully cut. Even worse, it meant that the total area of the wings would be reduced by about thirty-five square feet. That, of course, would upset his calculations. But since there was no other way, he settled for the shorter lengths and prepared to go to Elizabeth City.

After storing his things in Elizabeth City, Wilbur went in search of someone to take him across Albemarle Sound to Kitty Hawk. The usual response to his query was, ''Kitty Hawk? Hain't never heard o' that.''

Although the natives knew nothing about Kitty Hawk, the more colorful chapters of their history were on many tongues. Many spoke of Sir Walter Raleigh and the Lost Colony he founded on nearby Roanoke Island in 1585 as if the event were just a few years ago. They were also familiar with the exploits of the pirate, Edward Teach, better known as Blackbeard. "Used to sail these parts with his skull and crossbones flag a-flappin' from his mast," said an old-timer. "Ah, but his last voyage was one he didn't plan. A British sloop eventually got him and sailed up the James River with his head a-danglin' from the bowsprit."

After three days of futile search, Wilbur discovered a boatman by the name of Israel Perry who agreed to take him to Kitty Hawk. Delighted, Wilbur checked out of his hotel and piled his trunks on the nearest wharf. "But my boat ain't here," explained Perry. "It's three miles up the river." He pointed to a leaky skiff. "We'll put your things on that and then row over to the schooner on the coast."

As Perry and the deckhand rowed, Wilbur bailed. By the time they reached the flat-bottomed schooner on which Perry lived and fished, all of them were exhausted. As horrible as the skiff was, the schooner was much worse. It leaked. Its sails were in shreds. The rudderpost had rotted. Poorly tied ropes, many frayed, were scattered about the deck, and there were rats and insects all over its deck and in every crevice.

"It's forty miles to Kitty Hawk. Do you really think we can make the crossing in—in that?" asked Wilbur.

"Trust me."

By the time the boat was loaded, the sun had dropped below the horizon. While a pleasant breeze blew, Perry hoisted the sails and gradually pulled away from land. Suddenly the pleasant breeze began to blow harder, and then harder. Minutes later, the wind became a gale and the sails grew taut. Soon the ship was tossing. This motion increased until it seemed to stand on one end and then the other. Next, it began to roll and twist. Then the high waves poured inside.

Soon Wilbur and the other two were bailing water. But as frantically as they bailed, the water came in faster. Now, a new hazard struck. Rain. First it merely drizzled. Soon it was pouring. As Wilbur strained with his bucket, he heard a loud ripping sound. Looking up, he discovered the main sail had broken loose.

As the weather worsened, it seemed inevitable that they would drown. Then Perry showed that he was a skillful seaman. He jibed across the wind, got the wind to the rear, and managed to enter the shelter of a cove. Here, the trio, thankful that their lives had been saved, shivered on the deck till morning.

After some rest, the sails were repaired, and they set out again for Kitty Hawk. Although it still rained, the winds were more comfortable, the waves were fairly smooth, and there was no danger of sinking. It was dark by the time they made Kitty Hawk Bay. The few lights that burned in the area had been extinguished.

"Guess we'll have to wait her out till mornin'," said Perry.

Soaked and hungry, Wilbur lay down on the bare deck. But he could not sleep. It seemed that each board bit into his back. Then he remembered he was hungry. As his stomach churned, he removed the lid from a small jar of jelly Kate had persuaded him to accept. He had never eaten jelly by itself before; but now it was unusually good. When the jar was half empty, he replaced the lid and was soon asleep.

At dawn, with the help of Perry and the deckhand, Wilbur unloaded his things, paid his fare, and sat alone while he pondered over the location of William Tate's house, and how he would get there.

The morning sun was warm, and even though his clothes were like a drying mop, Wilbur felt better. In a few minutes, a boy by the name of Baum approached.

"I'm looking for William Tate's house," said Wilbur.

"Follow me," replied the boy. "It's 'bout a quarter of a mile down that-a-way. Say, are you that man who's gonna fly a glider?"

"I am." Wilbur swept his eyes over the wide beaches. "Does the wind blow much in these parts?"

"Shore does."

"How fast?"

"I—I really don't know. But there's a weather station over there. They'll know."

The Tate house was a two-story affair built of unplaned siding. At the door, Mrs. Tate and her daughter studied him with horrified stares. "Come in quick and get warm," said the mother. Her hair, pulled tightly around her head, was cotton-white, and her cone-shaped dress reached below her ankles. After she had opened the door, she added, "Looks like you're soaked and ain't had nothin' to eat for a long spell."

"All I've had for two days was a little jelly," confessed Wilbur.

"Well, you've come to the right place. Me and Bill have been a-waitin' fer you." She cracked three or four eggs into a heavy iron skillet and cut several slices of ham. "Maybe while I'm a-fixin' breakfast you'd like to change." She nodded toward a back room. "We've fixed a bed in there. Make yourself comfortable."

Clad in dry clothes, and sitting in the warm

kitchen with the tantalizing smell of ham and eggs and coffee about him, Wilbur looked around. The walls were bare of even plaster. There were no carpets or pictures and the ceiling was unvarnished pine. His eyes paused on the sewing machine. "Does it work?" he asked, pointing to the black treadle.

"Shore does. If you need it, he'p yo'self. How 'bout some hoe cake?"

"Sound's great."

After breakfast, Wilbur dried his wet suit, ironed it—and rested. The next morning he borrowed Tate's horse and cart and brought in his things from the wharf. Then, at a modest distance from the house, he erected his canvas lean-to. Here he worked on the glider.

Each piece of the machine had been cut to fit eighteen-foot spars; but since he had only sixteen-foot spars, numerous changes had to be made. As he placed each piece in the skeleton, he was extremely careful. Although the winds in the area were generally steady, sometimes they changed within a moment. Often, calms were followed by gusts. Thus, it was extremely important that the glider be strong enough to withstand violent change.

On September 23, ten days after his arrival in Kitty Hawk, Wilbur wrote to his father:

> I am staying with Mr. W.J. Tate, the postmaster at this place. . . . His occupation is fishing in the fishing season, which begins about Oct. 1st and lasts for about three months. . . . There may be one or two better houses here but his is much above average. . . .
>
> I have my machine nearly finished. It is not to have a motor and is not expected to fly. . . . My idea is to merely experiment and practice with a view to solving the problem of equilibrium. I have plans

which I hope to find much in advance of the methods
tried by previous experimenters. When once a
machine is under proper control under all conditions,
the motor problem will be quickly solved. A failure
of motor will then mean simply a slow descent & safe
landing instead of a disastrous fall.

The one thing Wilbur hadn't finished was that of
covering the wings with the sateen. This was like a
surgical operation and required great care. Carefully
he cut out a two-foot section in the center and then
spliced the sections together on Mrs. Tate's sewing
machine. Fortunately, the sock-like covering fit snugly
over the skeleton of each wing. Wilbur was completing
this task when a letter arrived from Orville saying that
he would be there soon.

Wilbur's younger brother arrived on September 28.
He had brought with him a large supply of food—
especially sugar—and a sizeable tent large enough to
house his brother and himself, together with the glider.
Likewise, he had a camera and a supply of
photographic plates.

After Wilbur had explained how he had been forced
to shorten each wing, Orville asked, "How many
square feet of wingspan do we have?"

"One hundred sixty-five square feet."

Orville got out his pencil. "We figured that since
the glider weighs fifty pounds and each of us one hundred forty pounds we'd need about two hundred
square feet of wingspan—that is about a foot for each
pound. How will we—"

"That'll be simple," interrupted Wilbur. "We'll
just fly it in faster winds."

Neither of the brothers were certain about the
proper camber that should be placed in the wings, nor
the point where that curve should start or reach its
highest peak. Lilienthal had believed that the camber

should be one-in-twelve. By that he meant that the peak of the curve should be one-twelfth of the *chord*— the width of the wing.

The camber of the wings the Wright brothers had made was one-in-twenty-two. While designing the glider in Dayton, Wilbur had no idea where the height of the camber should reach its maximum. He finally decided that it should be three inches from the front edge.

"Do you think that is correct?" asked Orville.

"We'll have to wait and see," replied Wilbur.

The next problem was to thread in the wire bracing for the wings, and to arrange the pulleys and cables so that the wings could be warped from a control center. But first, the five-foot struts had to be placed between the wings. Each strut was hinged on both ends so that it could be moved back and forth and thus warp the wings. Six of these uprights were placed in the front of each wing and six behind. The rear ones were placed about a foot from the wing edge.

After the wings were braced and the pulleys and warping cables arranged, the brothers attached a small elevator onto the front section. This elevator extended forward like the head and neck of a flying goose.

Lilienthal had always flown his gliders standing up. But remembering what their mother had taught them about air resistance, the Wrights had arranged their glider so that they could fly it while lying face down.

By Saturday morning, October 6, the glider was ready to be tested. Ropes had been attached to hold it down and others arranged so that the wings could be warped from the ground. Excited by the experiments they were about to perform, the brothers summoned Bill Tate to help them transport it to the testing place near the tower which they had erected.

Each brother lifted a wing by its tip while Tate supported the machine in the middle.

Wilbur was a little nervous as he watched Tate's beard blowing sideways in the wind. He and Orville had misunderstood the reports about the speed of winds in this area. The tables they had studied listed *average* speeds—not the extremes. Sometimes the winds were completely calm. At other times they whistled across the sands at sixty miles an hour.

As the trio cautiously moved forward, Orville kept glancing at the anemometer which he had borrowed from the Kitty Hawk weather station. It indicated that the wind was blowing at a rather hefty twenty-five miles an hour. The men settled the machine near the tower and gently held it in place. Then, each brother tested the warping ropes. Yes, the wings responded.

The great moment ending several years of work and study had come.

Slowly, Wilbur allowed the rope attached to the glider's nose to slip through his hands. Up, up it moved. When it was a little higher than their heads, it began to buck and prance. Wilbur had to strain on the rope to keep the glider from getting away. As he held on, Orville pulled and released the warping ropes. Again, each time the wings twisted, the glider responded.

"The warping works!" exclaimed Wilbur. "Now let's pull it down and let me get on board."

9

Failure

Wilbur crawled under the lower wing and wedged his body in an open space between the wings. Lying face downward, he found the warping lever with his feet. Then, elbows on each wing, he moved the lever back and forth with his feet. "Are the wings twisting?" he asked.

"They certainly are," replied Orville.

"Then let me rise."

As Orville slowly released the rope, the glider easily went up to a height of fifteen feet. Immediately it began to buck. Wilbur warped the wings. The machine responded, but the bucking continued. It was like riding a wild broncho.

Wilbur was terrified. "Lemme down!" he shouted. "Lemme down! Lemme down!"

Unable to hear because of the wind, Orville surmised that Wilbur wanted to go higher, so he let out more rope. This time Wilbur shouted even louder.

After he finally pulled him down, Orville asked, "What's the matter?"

"I told Pa that I'd be careful," replied Wilbur a little sheepishly.

After he had calmed down, Wilbur said, "Now I'll go up again, but please don't let me get much higher than the tops of your heads."

This time the glider was a little more calm. Again, Wilbur warped the wings. In addition, he adjusted the angle of the elevator. As he worked, gaining experience, he found that he was getting more and more control of the machine. After about half an hour of practice, he asked to be let down.

"Still frightened?" asked Orville.

"No. I'm now ready to go to the tower."

Wilbur was referring to a temporary tower he and Orville had erected in the nearby sands.

With a single rope from the glider tied securely to the top of the tower, Wilbur worked the controls while the machine shuddered and tugged, trying to get away. According to their figures, the nose of the glider should have remained at an upward pitch of about three degrees. Instead, it remained slanted upward at about twenty degrees! Puzzled, he asked Orville and Tate to pull him down. As he stood up and studied the situation, he said, "We must be doing something wrong."

"Maybe we miscalculated the tables," suggested Orville.

"I don't think so," murmured Wilbur. "It could be that our camber is wrong. Lilienthal's was one in twelve inches; ours is one in twenty-two inches."

"Could it be that the mesh in the cloth is not fine enough?"

Wilbur shook his head. "I have no idea. But let me go up again and try to figure it out." Riding the wind at the same height as before, Wilbur practiced with the controls. Then, suddenly, there was a thirty-mile-an-hour gust of wind. This time the nose went downward to an angle of about ten degrees. That was better. Still, something was drastically wrong.

Wilbur dismounted and tried to think of a solution. Then he went up again. After about three hours of this, he said, "Let's quit for the day." With Tate's help, Orville and Wilbur carried the glider back to their tent.

The next day being Sunday, the brothers took the day off to rest and think. Like their father, they respected the Lord's day.

The wind on Monday had slowed to twenty miles an hour. Since this was not enough to lift either of the brothers, they borrowed seventy-five pounds of chains from Mr. Tate and placed them in the spot where Wilbur had ridden between the lower wings. This weight was about all the glider could manage in the calmer wind.

"My figures say that with the wingspan we have, the glider should be able to carry twice that much weight," complained Wilbur.

"Then we've made a miscalculation," replied Orville.

Wilbur shook his head. "No, I was very careful with my figures."

"Could it be that Lilienthal and the others were wrong?"

Wilbur shrugged. "Perhaps. But I really doubt it. The Germans are great mathematicians. Still—maybe we'll have to figure out some way to make our own set of tables."

On Wednesday they let the glider fly from the tower on its own while they manipulated the wings and elevator with ropes from below. As they changed the warping and the elevator angles, they were both

surprised at the control they had achieved. Then disaster struck.

Having pulled the glider to the ground in order to make an adjustment to a rope, their eyes shifted from the glider. During that brief moment a gust of wind lifted the glider and slammed in onto the ground about twenty feet away. The brothers stared. In front of them was a pile of broken ribs and torn cloth.

"Well, that's the end of our experiments!" said Orville as he viewed the wreck before them. "It makes me sick."

Each was tempted to leave the glider where it was. But, almost instinctively, they gathered the pieces and took them to their tent. Perhaps their plight would seem better in the morning.

That night, both Orville and Wilbur found it hard to go to sleep. The problems of the glider kept slipping into their minds. Both were up at dawn, but as they poked through the debris they discovered that the wreck was not as bad as they had supposed. They had brought along numerous spare ribs and other parts for just such an emergency.

After breakfast, Orville and Wilbur got busy with their repairs. Mrs. Tate was generous with her sewing machine. With its help they got the sateen satisfactorily repaired. Each day, they took time off to walk along the beach. One morning they were stopped by a man.

"So yous are the ones that want to fly," he said. "Let me tells yous somethin'. God didn't make men to fly. He made 'em to rule the earth, not the sky." He pointed to some hawks and sea gulls soaring overhead. "If God wanted men to fly, He'd given 'em wings like them birds. Any man who wants to fly is as crazy as a bullbat."

Wilbur laughed. "Tell me, friend, why is this place called Kitty Hawk?" he asked as he studied the man's gap-toothed face.

"Ah really don't know. At least Ah'm not sure." The man rubbed his week-old whiskers. "But there's a story. Every year the coastal Injuns used to come in the fall to kill the migratin' geese which they called 'honks.' Because of that, they said that a white man's year was from 'Killy Honk to Killy Honk.' The whites then began to call the place Kitty Hawk." He shrugged. "At least it's a right smart story."

The man had started to leave when Wilbur motioned him back. "We've been thinking of gliding from Kill Devil Hills," he said. "Maybe you could tell us the reason for that name."

"Deed I can!" The man squared his shoulders. "Round a hundred years ago, a ship was wrecked over there." He pointed to whitecaps foaming near the beach. "A man was stationed to guard the wreck. One night he shot a prowler who'd come to steal. When the owners axed him 'bout it, he said, 'I killed that 'ol devil last night.' From then on the place is knowed as Kill Devil Hills.''

Wilbur and Orville worked hard getting the glider in condition to fly again. They were about finished when on October 15 a howling nor'wester began to blow. At night the winds whistled through the tent with such violence, both Wilbur and his brother had to get up and hold it by its seams to keep it from blowing away. While they were holding on, the top of the tent and the sides thundered like cattle whips.

By morning the wind had calmed. But sand was everywhere. On October 18th Orville addressed a letter to their sister. While sitting on an empty chicken coop, he wrote:

> We spent half the morning yesterday in getting the machine out of the sand. When we finally did get it free, we took it up the hill, and made a number of experiments in a 25 mile wind. . . . when we got through Will was so mixed up he couldn't even theorize. It has been with considerable effort that I have succeeded in keeping him in the flying business. . . . He likes to chase buzzards, thinking they are eagles. . . .

In spite of Orville's letter, Wilbur kept a close eye on the birds. He may have gotten their names mixed up, but he noted even the smallest details in their flights. In his book, *Miracle at Kitty Hawk*, Fred C. Kelly quoted at length from Wilbur's notebook written at this time:

> If a buzzard be soaring to leeward [away from the wind] of the observer, at a distance of a thousand feet, and a height of about one hundred feet, the cross section of its wings will be a mere line when the bird

is moving from the observer but when it moves toward him the wings will appear broad.

This would indicate that its wings are always inclined upward which seems contrary to reason.

Buzzards find it difficult to advance in the face of a wind blowing more than thirty miles an hour. Their soaring speed cannot be far from thirty miles.

Life at Kitty Hawk was not completely miserable; and, although most of the people considered the Wrights a little daft, some of the birds kept an interested eye on them. Orville wrote to Kate, "A mockingbird lives in a tree that overhangs our tent. He is very tame, and perches on the highest bow of the tree (which however is only about ten feet high) and calls us up every morning. I think he crows up especially early after every storm to see whether we are still here."

Wilbur and Orville were agreed that they would leave Kitty Hawk for Dayton on October 23. "But before we leave," said Wilbur, "I must see what it's like to glide."

With the help of Tate, the brothers carried the glider the approximate three miles from their camp to the main Kill Devil Hill. Wilbur glanced at the one-hundred-foot-tall sand hill. "Now if we'll take it to the top, and if the wind's right, we can make a few glides."

The anemometer indicated that the wind was blowing at twelve miles an hour. "If we move into the wind, the speed of the glider, plus the speed of the wind, will give us enough lift," said Wilbur. The glider in position, Wilbur climbed inside. Ready for the test, he said, "First, just lift it up about a foot and then let it drop."

As Orville and Tate lifted the wings by their ends, Wilbur held his breath. At a signal, the glider was dropped. It touched the sand and moved forward a few feet. After spitting out some fine sand, Wilbur said, "All right, now let's do it again."

After several successful drops Wilbur was ready. This time Orville and Tate lifted the machine and ran forward about one hundred yards. Then they shouted, "You're free." Wilbur responded by immediately adjusting the elevator. The glider reacted by rising three feet into the air. Wilbur felt a tingling sensation racing down his spine. *He, Wilbur Wright, was flying!* He was tempted to lift the elevator a little more and thus rise higher. But with amazing self-control he let it stay where it was. The flight continued for about one hundred feet. When the glider touched the sand it skidded forward for a few feet. Nothing was damaged.

Wilbur climbed out from under the wings. After spitting out some more fine sand, he said, "It was wonderful. How fast do you think I was going?"

"Since the wind was blowing at twelve miles an hour, you were probably moving at thirty miles an hour" replied Orville. "That means that you were crossing the sand at eighteen miles an hour."

"Well, I'm ready to try it again," said Wilbur.

After another dozen flights, each a successful one, the brothers, together with the help of Mr. Tate, carried the machine back to camp.

Since the Wrights were through with this glider, they gave it to the Tates. Mrs. Tate saved the sateen to make a dress for her daughter, and Mr. Tate used the rest of the glider for fuel. Thus, the machine that had cost fifteen dollars to build came to an end. Wilbur and Orville felt that their trip had been a failure. Still, they had learned many things and were determined to return the next year for additional experiments.

While they were waiting for transportation at

Elizabeth City on October 23, Wilbur wrote a brief letter to his sister. Affecting the local dialect, he scribbled: "We have said Good-bye Kitty. Good-bye Hawk. Good-bye Kitty Hawk. We're gwine to leave you now. We reached here this afternoon after a pleasant trip from Kitty Hawk of six hours."

10

Back to Kitty Hawk

Shortly after Orville and Wilbur arrived in Dayton, Katherine decided that the family should celebrate their safe return with a special dinner. Both Carrie and Katherine donned newly starched aprons and went to work. As they were preparing the roast, Wilbur stepped into the kitchen.

"Go back into the other room," ordered Kate. "You're a guest!"

"Maybe so. But I'm starved for gravy and it must be just right."

"Don't you trust us?" asked Carrie.

"For ordinary things, yes. But for gravy, no. Now, if you'll pardon me, I'll get busy. Where's the sieve?"

After Bishop Wright had said grace, he asked, "Was your trip really worthwhile? Do you still believe that men will fly?"

"There's no doubt about it," replied Orville as he poured the rich brown gravy over his potatoes. "They will fly. But we have a lot to learn."

"About how long were you in the air?" pressed their father.

"Wilbur was up in the glider when we flew it as a kite many times," replied Orville. "But he only spent a few seconds in actual flight."

Bishop Wright frowned. "Do you think the trip was worth all that trouble if you only flew for a few moments?" he asked.

Wilbur and Orville stared at each other for a long time in silence. Then, as Orville buttered a slice of bread, he replied, "In a way, yes; and in a way, no. We did prove that our warping idea works. But—" He sighed. "But, Pa, there are a lot of problems that have to be worked out."

That afternoon Orville decided that his greatest need was for a large pan of fudge. Apron on, he mixed the ingredients, and then carefully tested the mixture with a long thermometer he had secured for just that purpose.

During his first few days at home Wilbur was a little discouraged, but as he considered what they had learned, his enthusiasm gradually returned. Soon, he began to correspond with Octave Chanute. In the back of his mind he was planning a new glider and a second trip to Kitty Hawk. Worried about the bicycle business which they needed to support them, the brothers employed Charles Taylor to manage their business. Taylor had been earning fifteen dollars a week from the Dayton Electric Company. They paid him eighteen dollars a week.

Taylor was about Wilbur's age and he had a thorough knowledge of machinery, including the new combustion engines that were just being developed. This last qualification especially interested the Wrights, for they were already dreaming of putting a gasoline-powered motor on a glider. Taylor loved his work and often put in twelve to eighteen hours a day.

During almost every spare moment, Orville and Wilbur argued and made drawings of a new glider. This one had to have a wider wingspan. The camber, too, would be different. Instead of the curve being one inch for every twenty-two inches of the breadth of the wing, as in their first glider, the new wings would be curved in the same manner as those of Lilienthal. That is, the curve would be one inch to twelve inches of breadth. However, they decided that the peak of the curve would be a little behind the one used by Lilienthal. (At the time, neither brother realized that a change of one eighth of an inch could make a vast difference.)

Although both Wilbur and Orville were concentrating on the mysteries of gliding, they also had time for other things. One time when the bishop was on a trip, Kate wrote to him, "Orv has begun lessons on his mandolin and we are getting even with the neighbors for the noise they have made on their pianos. He sits around and picks on that thing until I can hardly stay in the house."

The new glider had a wingspan of twenty-two feet, and the wings were seven feet across. Counting both wings, this meant that they had a wing area of over three hundred square feet. The entire machine weighed ninety-eight pounds, and was thus the largest and heaviest glider built up to that time.

Since it would be difficult to house this machine in a tent, the brothers decided that they would need a shed in which to store it. Carefully they designed an adequate shelter and sent orders ahead to a lumberyard with instructions to forward the pieces to Kitty Hawk. About a week before they were to leave Dayton, a letter arrived from Octave Chanute.

The engineer's letter explained that his assistant, E. C. Huffacker, had just built a glider for him out of paper tubing, and that he would like to test it at Kitty Hawk. He suggested that Huffacker would help them with their testing if they would help him with his testing.

Neither of the Wrights were enthusiastic about the idea, but they agreed for him to come. Then Chanute had another idea. He was alarmed at them in performing dangerous experiments without nearby medical aid available. He suggested that they allow him to send along George Spratt, a medical graduate who had given up medicine for aeronautics. Again, the Wrights were a little unhappy about this intrusion, but they agreed for him to come; and, in addition, they invited Chanute to spend some time with them.

"Looks like we'll have a merry lot," grumbled Wilbur.

As they were making their final preparations to leave for North Carolina, Wilbur received two magazines in the mail—one from England and another from Germany. He had a brief article on gliding in each of them. Then, as he was rejoicing, the June issue of *Cassier's Magazine* was dropped in their mailbox. Since this was a leading journal aimed at American engineers, Wilbur eagerly picked it up. Moments later, he exclaimed, "Look, Orv, Chanute has an article in this issue and he's mentioned us. Listen!" He read:

> Since these experiments [Chanute's] a further advance has been achieved by Messrs. Wilbur and Orville Wright, who have produced a double-deck gliding machine in which the operator is placed in a horizontal position, thus opposing to forward motion one square foot instead of five square feet . . . and they have further reduced the resistance

of the framing by adopting improved shapes, so that the aggregate head resistances are reduced to about half of those which previously obtained.

When Wilbur and Orville arrived at Elizabeth City on July 8 a furious storm was brewing. "The weather's just like last year," grumbled Wilbur as they checked into their hotel. "Look at those clouds!"

"Maybe it'll be over by morning," suggested Orville.

The next day the storm was whistling with a constantly increasing violence. It bent trees and hurled everything that was loose. The windows in the hotel rattled. At the weather station the anemometer cups broke down when they reached 97 miles per hour. (In a nearby city the anemometer reached 107 miles per hour.)

It was the worst storm in that area on record.

"Do you think the Lord's telling us to go home?" asked Wilbur.

Orville frowned. "Of course not!" But even as he spoke, large trees were being uprooted.

In spite of the fury, the brothers waited until there was a moderate calm. Then they continued on to Kitty Hawk and arrived there on July 11. They spent their first night with the Tates.

Again the heavy iron skillet sizzled with thick slices of ham and eggs. As they were eating, Wilbur turned to Tates' daughter. "How do you like the dress your ma made out of our glider?" he asked.

"Oh, fine," she said blushing.

"Does it ever fly?"

She laughed. "In winds like this I can hardly keep it down!"

Although it was still raining on the twelfth, the brothers hauled their large tent to Kill Devil Hill.

"Aren't you gonna wait until the rain stops?" asked Tate.

Wilbur smiled. "We'd like to," he said, pulling on his raincoat, "but I'm afraid we don't have a minute to spare."

By the time they got the tent up, however, the rain was so heavy they had to stay inside for three days. Eventually the storm calmed, and since they had carefully planned their shed, it was soon erected. Wilbur described their experiences in a letter to Kate.

> After fooling around all day inside the tent, excepting on a few occasions when we rushed out to drive a few more tent pegs, our thirst became unbearable. . . . Oh misery! Most dead for water and none within a mile! excepting that which was coming from the skies. However, we decided to catch a little of this, and placed the dishpan where the water dripped down from the tent roof; and though it tasted somewhat of the soap which we had rubbed on the canvas . . . it pretty well filled a longfelt want.
>
> Sunday night I was taken sick and 'most died,' that is I felt as if I did.
>
> Mr. Juffaker arrived Thursday afternoon, and with him a swarm of mosquitoes.

There were so many mosquitoes "the sand and grass and trees and hills and everything was fairly covered with them." Wilbur continued with his letter to Kate:

> They chewed us clear through our underwear and socks. Lumps began swelling all over my body like hen's eggs. . . . We put our cots out under the awnings and wrapped up in our blankets with only our noses protruding from the folds. . . . The wind which had been blowing over twenty miles an hour, dropped off entirely. Our blankets then became unbearable. The perspiration . . . (rolled) off . . .

in torrents. We would uncover and the mosquitoes would sweep down on us in vast multitudes. . . . Misery! Misery! The half can never be told. . . .

The next night we constructed mosquito frames and nets over our cots. [Soon] the tops of the canopies were covered with mosquitoes till there was hardly standing room. . . . The buzzing was like the buzzing of a mighty buzz saw. . . . Affairs had now become so desperate that it began to look as if camp would have to be abandoned or we [would] perish.

The next day they dragged in old stumps from up to a quarter of a mile away. They placed the stumps in a circle around the camp, and set them on fire. Perhaps the smoke would discourage the mosquitoes. This plan was only a partial success.

Mr. Spratt, who had now joined the group, decided that the mosquitoes were better than the smoke. He boldly dragged his bed out into the open. Soon Wilbur and Orville heard him slapping mosquitoes. *Wham! Bam! Wham! Wham!* Each of the brothers had to hold his nose to keep from laughing. Still, the fight continued, only now their new guest added words to his slaps: "Take that, you little devils! And that, and that, and that!"

After a twenty-minute battle, Spratt gave up. As he dragged his bed back to camp, he muttered half aloud to himself, "I'd rather suffocate with smoke than be eaten alive by mosquitoes!"

When the camp had quieted, Wilbur whispered to Orville, "Do you think that learning to fly is worth all this trouble?"

"Of course!" replied Orville.

After a long quiet, Wilbur whispered, "I'm not sure that it is. Maybe we'll fail."

"We don't have anything to complain about. Neither of us has been hurt. Remember when Otto

Lilienthal was dying after breaking his neck in his gliding accident, he said, '*Opfer m*üssen gebracht werden!' ''

"And that means 'sacrifices must be made,' " interpreted Wilbur. "But haven't we suffered enough?"

Orville laughed. "At least we're still alive!"

Wilbur's only reply was to slap at a mosquito that had broken the smoke barrier and was drilling for blood on the end of his nose.

George Spratt and the Wright brothers admired one another. But Spratt was concerned about the one-in-twelve-inch camber in the new Wright glider. "It will be very unstable, perhaps even dangerous," he said.

Wilbur shrugged. "We've followed the formula put together by Lilienthal and others," he said. "Still, there's only one way to learn the truth, and that is to experiment!"

With the help of his guests and brother, Wilbur cautiously carried their new glider halfway up the Big Kill Devil Hill. Two years later Wilbur described the mounds of sand known as Kill Devil Hills in a lecture before the Western Society of Engineers. He said:

> The practice ground at the Kill Devil Hills consists of a level plain of bare sand, from which rises a group of detached hills or mounds formed of sand heaped up by the winds. These hills are constantly changing in height and slope, according to the direction and force of the prevailing winds. The three which we use for gliding experiments are known as the Big Hill, the Little Hill and the West Hill, and have heights of 100 feet, 30 feet and 60 feet.

That Saturday morning, July 27, the wind was blowing at only ten miles an hour. This was five miles an hour less than what was needed to fly the glider as a kite. It was for this reason the brothers decided to experiment with gliding.

With the glider positioned ready to go, Wilbur climbed into the prepared place on the lower wing. He knew that he should position himself so that his center of gravity would match that of the glider. But where was that point? He didn't know. Positioned where he guessed it to be, he gave the signal to his helpers. The men lifted the glider about two feet, ran forward, and let it go. The machine remained in the air for a few yards and then settled down. No damage was done, but Wilbur was disappointed.

"I will move back a few inches and then we can try it again," said Wilbur.

The next try did not succeed because the lower wing scraped the top of a miniature sand dune.

On the ninth try, the glider stayed above the sand for about a yard and continued in the air for a little over three hundred feet. Orville was delighted. But Wilbur shook his head.

"There's something wrong, Orv," commented Wilbur thoughtfully as he crawled out to view the machine. "I had to push the elevator into extreme positions to keep it in the air, and to keep it from rising too high. We're going to have to make some changes."

After the glider had been taken back up to its starting place for the tenth time, Wilbur crawled into place again. Now he was lying a full foot behind the position he had taken on his first glide.

This time the glider moved three or four feet above the sand and continued this way for about one hundred feet, then it slowly began to rise higher and higher. Soon, it was ten feet high, then twenty, and then thirty. As Wilbur viewed the sand getting lower and then lower, one of the helpers began to race beneath him.

"Be careful! Be careful!" shouted the man, waving his arms.

Wilbur realized that he was in the same position Lilienthal had been in when a gust of wind changed the center of balance in his glider and it had nosed down, breaking his neck. But what was he to do?

Wilbur prayed, pushed the elevator to its most positive position, and changed the center of gravity by inching himself forward a few inches. His moves had just the right effect. The glider landed safely. After he had crawled out and stood up he was jubilant. "The elevator works!" he exclaimed.

Still, he was not satisfied.

Thoughtfully, Wilbur walked all around the glider, viewing it from every angle. Shaking his head, he muttered, "Orv, I'm convinced that Lilienthal's tables are wrong. We're going to have to make new ones. Big as they are, our wings don't have enough lift."

"Make new tables? But how?" asked Orville.

"I don't know. Still, Ma used to say, 'Knock and it shall be opened unto you.' Well, I'm going to keep knocking!"

Having decided to alter the camber of the wings, the brothers "proceeded to truss down the ribs of the whole machine, so as to reduce the depth of the curvature," remembered Wilbur. Also they fastened a long spar across the front of the wing. In a crude way this changed the camber from one in twelve, to one in twenty.

The next Thursday, August 8, the glider was returned to Big Kill Devil Hill and Wilbur mounted it for another glide. This time the longitudinal control was vastly improved. "It guides much better," exulted Wilbur.

Altogether, Wilbur made thirteen flights that day. The longest one was four hundred feet. On each occasion he was able to keep the glider a mere three or four feet above the sand, and to set it down gracefully.

That evening as the men wolfed down their evening meal, the discussion centered on learning to turn the glider in midflight. Octave Chanute had now joined the group and there was a lively discussion. Each agreed that when a bird banked in the air, one wing moved a little higher than the other.

"This we can do by warping the wings," said Wilbur.

The next day the sun was bright, the anemometer registered a comfortable twenty-mile-an-hour wind, and each man was anxious for new tests. This time, they carried the glider almost to the top of Big Kill Devil Hill.

"Ready?" asked Orville.

"Ready," replied Wilbur from his prone position.

Safely in the air, Wilbur warped the wings. There was an instant response and Wilbur glowed with joy. But as the glider curved, he became aware of a new instability. He adjusted the controls. There was little response. True, the glider turned. Still—although puzzled, he managed a safe landing.

On his fifth flight that day, Wilbur became aware of increasing instability. Then the left wing dipped far too deeply. Frantically he pushed the elevator control. He was too late. The tip of the left wing bit into the sand and he was hurled forward against the canvas elevator.

Breathing heavily, Wilbur examined himself. Other than a bruised nose and a black eye, he was all right. The glider, too, suffered only a few easily-repairable injuries.

Somewhat discouraged, the entire group spent Saturday and Sunday resting. No one, not even

Chanute, could pinpoint the problem. On Monday and Tuesday, Wilbur made a number of seven-second glides. These flights, however, offered no clue to the problem. In his notes, Wilbur wrote, "Upturned wing seems to fall behind, but at first it rises."

The birds all knew the secret of turning while in flight. But their secret was so deep no one could solve it. That Thursday the discouraged brothers boarded the train that would take them back to Dayton. Instead of being excited about going home, the brothers were unusually silent. Even the toneless, "tickets please," of the fat conductor failed to arouse them. Their world had collapsed.

Back in Dayton, following supper, Wilbur stared out the window and mumbled, "You know, Orv, men will not fly in our lifetime." He swatted a mosquito. "No, they won't even fly in a thousand years!" He slapped another mosquito and walked away.

Viewing her brothers, Kate sensed things had not gone well at Kitty Hawk. Neither had even requested brown gravy! A few days later, Bishop Wright scribbled in his diary, "The boys walked in unexpectedly on Thursday . . . haven't said a word about flying."

Orville and Wilbur's gloom continued to darken. Then an article by Simon Newcomb, Ph.D., LL.D., in the September issue of *McClure's* pushed them even deeper into the muck of despair. Under the title, *Is the Airship Coming?*, the brilliant astronomer wrote:

> If we had metal so rigid . . . that a sheet of it twenty meters square and a millimeter thick would be as stiff as a board and weigh not more than a ton, and, at the same time, so strong, that a powerful engine could be built of little weight, we might hope for a flying machine that would carry a man. But as the case stands, the first successful flyer will be the work of a watchmaker, and will carry nothing heavier than an insect.

Wilbur read the article several times. Then he took it to Orville. "Look at this," he exclaimed. "This super-smart doctor says that the first flying machine will be built by a watchmaker and that his first passenger will be no heavier than an insect. What do you think of that?"

Orville read the article, then he tossed the magazine on the table. "I don't think much of it," he said, speaking thoughtfully. "Newcomb may know about the moons of Jupiter, but he doesn't know anything about air currents—especially those at Kitty Hawk, North Carolina!"

The Wind Tunnel

Trying to dismiss flying from their minds, Wilbur and Orville spent their time at the bicycle shop. Charles Taylor was puzzled by their attitudes. He missed their arguments.

In the midst of this silence about flying machines. Wilbur received a letter, dated August 29, 1901, from Octave Chanute. After a startled reading, he turned to his brother. "Listen to this, Orv," he said. He then read from the letter:

> I have been talking with some members of the Western Society of Engineers. The conclusion is that the members would be very glad to have an address, or a lecture from you, on your gliding experiments. We have a meeting on the 18th of September. . . . If you conclude to come I hope you will do me the favor of stopping at my house. We should have the photos you want to use about a week before the lecture in order to get lantern slides. The more the better.

"What do you think of that?" asked Wilbur.

"I think it's wonderful!"

"But I don't have the proper clothes." Wilbur frowned. "There'll be a lot of highfalutin' people there!"

"Nonsense, Will. I'll lend you mine."

"Mmmmm. Mmmmm." Wilbur paced around and rubbed his chin. "We do have plenty of pictures, and some of 'em are pretty good. But to have to lecture to all of those famous people. No, it's impossible!"

Orville stared at his brother with a look of scorn. "You've taught Sunday school, and you were going to be a preacher. Besides, our father's a bishop!"

"Oh, all right. But I'll have to get busy. I don't have much time." He frowned, got to his feet, and stepped through the door.

Working late, Wilbur produced a ten thousand word lecture that seemed satisfactory to Orville. In it, Wilbur told about their flights, what they had observed, and their disappointments. He was quite frank, but when he came to those points in which he and Orville had made discoveries, he was careful to speak in only general terms. After all, they were already talking about patenting their system of warping the wings.

The entire family cooperated in seeing that Wilbur was properly dressed. From Orville, he borrowed an overcoat, shirt, cuff links, and collars. As Wilbur preened before the mirror, the entire group made comments. "The shirt needs a little more starch. That tie doesn't quite match. Those cuff links could stand a little polish. Here, let me go over those shoes again."

The final verdict from the family and even Carrie was that he looked "swell."

"Clothes make the man!" concluded Kate with a decisive toss of her head.

After being introduced by Chanute, Wilbur began his lecture. At first he was a little nervous, but an opening demonstration soon pulled the people to the edge of their seats. Holding a sheet of blank paper in his outstretched hand, he said, "If I take this piece of paper, and after placing it parallel to the ground, quickly let it fall, it will not settle down as a staid, sensible piece of paper ought to do, but it insists on contravening every recognized rule of decorum, turning over and darting hither and thither in the most erratic manner, much after the style of an untrained horse."

He then dropped the paper and it did precisely what he had said it would do. After it had settled to the floor, he continued, "Yet this is the style of steed that men must learn to manage before flying can become an everyday sport. The bird has learned this art of equilibrium, and learned it so thoroughly that its skill is not apparent in our sight."

From this introduction, Wilbur explained how he and Orville were attempting to learn to fly. "Now there are two ways of learning how to ride a fractious horse. One way is to get on him and learn by actual practice how each motion and trick may best be met; the other is to sit on a fence and watch the beast a while, and then retire to the house and at leisure figure out the best way of overcoming his jumps and kicks. The latter system is the safest; but the former, on the whole, turns out the larger proportion of good riders. It is very much the same in learning to ride a flying machine; if you are looking for perfect safety, you will do well to sit on a fence and watch the birds; but if you really wish to learn, you must mount a machine and become acquainted with its tricks by actual trial."

Wilbur went into the history of his and Orville's experiments. He was generous with his credit to others. "Herr Otto Lilienthal seems to have been the first man who really comprehended that balancing was the *first* instead of the *last* of the great problems in connection with human flight. He began where others left off."

Having praised Lilienthal, however, Wilbur went on to show that his hero had been mistaken in his tables about camber and airlift.

That evening as Wilbur was preparing to retire, his host, Octave Chanute, was lavish with his praise. "I was especially interested," he said, "in your statement that in time gliders would be able to 'maintain themselves for hours in the air.' I would like to publish your lecture in our society's *Journal*."

"I am flattered," replied Wilbur, "but first I want to make certain that my statements can be proved. I want to think of a way in which we can test lifting power of various curves. Orville and I have a lot of work ahead of us. In time, we want to design wings that will work as well as those of birds." He shook his head. "My brother and I have a lot of work ahead of us."

On his way back to Dayton, Wilbur's enthusiasm continued to grow. Deep inside, he was certain the Lord would lead him to the correct solutions.

Upon his return to Dayton, the entire family greeted him with glowing enthusiasm. "I'm proud of you," said their father. "Jesus told us to seek truth, and that's what you're doing."

Finding Wilbur sitting at the table and drawing bird wings, Kate asked, "Are you taking drawing lessons?"

"No. I'm just studying the curvature of various bird wings. The top one is that of a Gray Pelican. Notice that it is a little deeper than that of the Herring Gull. And see, this buzzard's wing is quite shallow. Also, it is longer than any of the others.''

"Why is that?''

"I don't know. But I'm going to find out. I'm convinced that the secret of flying is tied up in the general design of birds. The Lord made some of them so that they can soar for hours. Others, like chickens, for example, can barely fly. You should see the birds at Kitty Hawk! There are thousands of them. Ah, but I wish they'd tell me their secrets!''

As he pondered how he could measure the lift of variously shaped curves, Wilbur suddenly had an idea. He took an ordinary bicycle wheel, bolted a letter-envelope-sized plate on the edge of the rim, and then mounted another one with a curve in it 120 degrees away. He placed this wheel in a horizontal position in front of the handlebars.

"That's a strange place for a spare wheel,'' commented Bishop Wright.

Wilbur laughed. "It's not a spare wheel, Pa,'' he replied. "As you can see, it has a curved plate on one side and a straight one on the other side. When I ride the bicycle into the wind, I'll see which way the wheel turns. Then I'll exchange the curved plate with another which has a different amount of curve. I'll keep doing this until I find the curve which has the greatest lift.''

"Good idea, Will. But—'' The bishop viewed the wheel from several angles. Then, pinching his whiskers, he had a question. "What if the wind blows harder on one side than on the other?''

Wilbur studied his father for a long moment. "You've made a good point,'' he replied at last. "Orv and I will find a solution.''

Eyes on the horizontal wheel, Wilbur rode the

bicycle on both windy and calm days. Often as he rode by a crowd of people, he noticed their puzzled faces as they glimpsed his tireless, horizontal wheel. Many shrugged. One old man remarked, "Always thought them Wright kids a little daft. Now I know'd it!"

Convinced that due to the varying pressures of the wind on either side of the wheel, his readings would not be accurate, Wilbur pondered over a method that would improve the accuracy of his measurements. As he turned over one idea and then another, his eyes were suddenly drawn to a weathervane on the roof of a barn.

Yes, that was the answer!

Wilbur secured a weathervane and removed the wide, fishtailed, vertical fin. In its place, he bolted the curved piece in such a way that air pressure would move it to the right. Next, he attached the straight piece and adjusted it so that air pressure would move it to the left. His idea was that one plate working against the other would indicate the airlift of the curved piece. Then, in order that he might have an even air pressure, he placed this apparatus toward the end of a long wooden trough with a flat bottom.

With a fan blowing at one end of the trough, Wilbur watched the movement of the weathervane. Having pasted discarded wallpaper at the bottom of the trough, he marked how the weathervane responded to each separate curved piece. As he worked, he was almost startled. In a long letter to Chanute, dated October 6, he wrote, "I am now absolutely certain that Lilienthal's table is very seriously in error."

He then went on in a technical way to describe to Chanute some of his findings:

> The results obtained, with the rough apparatus used, were so interesting in their nature, and gave evidence of such possibility of exactness in measuring the value of $P_{(tang. \ a)}/P_{90}$, that we decided to construct an apparatus giving the value of $P_{(tang. \ a)}/P_{90}$ at all angles up to 30° and for surfaces of different curvatures and different relative lengths and breadths.

Encouraged by what they had learned from the bicycle wheel and the weathervane, the Wrights built a much more accurate device—a wind tunnel. By coincidence, Dr. A. F. Zahm of Washington D. C. also built a wind tunnel. His was forty feet long, six feet square, and had windows in the sides and on the top. This huge aisle-like affair was powered by a five-foot suction fan that *drew* the air through the enclosed structure.

In contrast to this expensive tunnel, that of the Wrights was quite simple. It was six feet long, sixteen inches square, and was almost entirely constructed out of scrap material. There was a single window at the top. The wind was blown through the tunnel by means of an engine which they designed and built for themselves. Since they wanted the wind to be uniform throughout the tunnel, a "wind-straightener" in the form of a parallel set of vanes was set immediately in front of the fan.

Then, under the window, where they could be observed, Wilbur and Orville arranged bars on which perfectly flat plates were suspended. The curved pieces to be tested were firmly secured above these. Thus, when the wind blew, the curved pieces worked against the flat pieces and so indicated the amount of "lift" which they possessed.

In order that their measurements be as accurate as possible, no large item was ever moved in the room where the apparatus had been set up.

During the next two months, over two hundred potential wings were tested. These wings—curved pieces—were cut from sheet metal.

As the brothers worked, they continued to argue. Often their arguments became near-shouting matches; and, as they raised their voices, they waved their hands and arms. Sometimes their hands made crash landings, at other times they made sharp turns to the left or right. Since Kate knew little about camber, chord, drag, lift, tangentials, ascensional force, she seldom knew what the conflict was about. But once she got so disturbed she put her fingers in her ears and shouted, "If you don't stop arguing I'll move!"

Charles Taylor also became concerned. He remembered, "Both had tempers, but no matter how angry they got, I never heard them use a profane word. . . . They'd shout at each other something terrible. I don't think they really got mad, but they sure got awfully hot." Nonetheless, their arguments produced data. This they arranged in charts. They mailed these to Chanute who, in turn, mailed back his criticism.

As the inventors worked, they became more and more convinced that Otto Lilienthal's tables were in drastic error. They also discovered the reason the first helicopter they had built wouldn't fly.

"And why wouldn't it fly?" asked Kate at breakfast. "And please tell me in simple language so that I can understand!"

"It wouldn't fly," explained Orville patiently, "because it was twice as big as the one Pa brought home. Being twice as big it needed *eight* times as much power."

Octave Chanute was so impressed with the progress of the Wright brothers he suggested to them that he might be able to persuade a rich man to send them ten thousand dollars a year, and thus enable them to spend their full time in aircraft research. "I happen to know Carnegie. Would you like for me to write to him?"

"How about it, Orv?" asked Wilbur.

"I'm not interested. We'll succeed on our own."

They both laughed.

With this fresh data before them, the Wrights designed a new glider. The wings were now thirty-two feet and one inch from tip to tip. Each wing was only five feet wide and thus the narrowest they had ever used. Also, the curvature was one inch in twenty-four inches. This was the shallowest they had ever tried. Another change was the distance of the peak of the curve from the front of the wing. This time they placed it twenty inches from the forward edge of the wing. Thus the high place was far behind that of their former gliders.

The method of control was also changed. Instead of warping the wings with a foot lever, a cradle was installed which allowed the operator to twist the wings with his hips as he lay stretched out over the lower wing.

The space between the upper and lower wings remained at just under five feet. This distance had seemed about right on the older gliders, so they didn't see any advantage in changing it.

Strangely, even though the birds they studied had tails, the Wrights hadn't seen the necessity of putting a tail on their gliders. Now, they decided to experiment. This new glider would have a tail! The tail they constructed was a vertical one, made of two vanes parallel to each other. Each vane was six feet tall and one foot wide.

"Maybe this tail will solve our turning problem," said Wilbur.

Altogether, the new glider weighed 112 pounds. Both brothers were confident that success was just ahead. Orville's diary records what happened next.

Wednesday, August 27, 1902
Started for Kitty Hawk at 3:45 A.M. . . . Anchored at 4:00 P.M. Slept on deck.

Friday, August 29, 1902
Spent day in arranging kitchen and driving 16-foot well. Building sank about two feet each end.

Saturday, August 30, 1902
Set up bicycle. Fixed up table & upholstered seat. Will took trip to Kitty Hawk on bicycle, bring(ing) back can of oil with him.

Thursday, September 5, 1902
Put on tar-paper roofing. O.W. sick. In bed most of day. Saw buzzard soar on north side of Big Hill, standing in one position.

The enthusiastic Wrights were prepared to stay for three, or even four months. One way or another, they were going to learn the mysteries of flying.

The buzzards had mocked them long enough!

The Story of a Tail

Working feverishly, the Wrights finished attaching the tail to their glider on Friday, September 19, at 10:30 A.M.

"It looks nice," said Dan Tate, William Tate's half-brother, whom they had hired to help with their experiments.

"It's ready to fly," said Orville. "But first we must have dinner." (Their mother had taught them the power of method and routine, and they refused to change.)

Food eaten, dishes washed and put away, the Wrights were ready. Still, there was another delay. Photographs! After taking two pictures of the glider as they were flying it as a kite, Dan Tate helped the brothers take the glider to a small hill. There, they made about twenty-five short glides.

The Wrights were not completely satisfied with the results. "But," as Orville wrote in his diary, "we are convinced that the trouble with the 1901 machine is overcome by the vertical tail.'' Both were anxious to try some real glides from the big hill the next day.

''I hope the weather is just right,'' said Wilbur that night—just before he slipped into bed.

The wind the next morning, Saturday, September 20, was blowing steadily at about eighteen miles an hour. Wilbur was delighted. ''Today is *the* day!'' he exclaimed. ''If all goes well, I want you to start training to fly.''

''I'm ready,'' replied Orville.

With Dan Tate's help, the trio carried the glider to about the center of the hill. ''Aren't we going to the top?'' asked Tate.

''Not this time,'' explained Wilbur. ''Before I make a major glide with turns, I want to make a few straight hops.'' He then crawled into the space reserved for the pilot and made certain that his hips were snug in the cradle. Then, after he had warped the wings a few times by twisting to the right and then to the left, he said, ''I'm ready.''

Helped by Tate, who lifted the right wing, Orville lifted the left wing. Both men ran forward. Soon the glider was in the air. Wilbur was overjoyed. The machine had much better lift than the previous ones. *Yes, their new tables were at least an improvement over those of Lilienthal!*

After a safe landing, Wilbur wiped the sand from his face. Then he said, ''Everything is working well. But I think I should make several other short glides before I try a big one and attempt a few turns.''

The next glide was started from a little higher up the hill, and the next one higher, and each of the following higher yet. But Wilbur was not completely satisfied. Occasionally the glider trembled, seeming to attempt to get out of control. *What was the reason*

*for those mysterious twists and shudders? Was it the wind,
or was he doing something wrong?*

During the next flight, Wilbur attempted a gentle
turn. The glider responded; and from the ground he
could hear the loud cheers of both Orville and Dan
Tate. Wilbur was happy, and yet—

"Now I want to glide from the very top of the hill,"
he announced after he had settled the machine on the
sand below. "Perhaps in a longer flight I'll have the
time to learn what's wrong."

The flight from the top of the hill went well for about
two hundred feet. Then suddenly the left wing twisted
upward and an unseen force slapped at his body. It
was as if he were being swatted by the hockey stick
again. Had it not been for his snug fit in the cradle
he would have been slammed onto the ground.
Desperately he tried to regain control. Instinctively,
he pushed with his right foot, having forgotten that
the foot control had been transferred to the cradle.

As Wilbur struggled for control, the glider slipped
sideways, the right wing struck the ground, and the
machine pivoted around before slapping the earth in
a flat position. Fortunately, Wilbur had kept his arm
around a strut. This support and the protection of the
elevator kept him from being killed.

Within seconds Orville was at his side. Wilbur was
still for only a moment. Sitting up, he said, "The
machine's all right. I just forgot and did the wrong
thing."

Fortunately, the glider was not seriously damaged.

After gaining his breath, Wilbur said, "Let's go
to the top of the hill again. I need to get some more
experience."

Dan Tate and Orville exchanged glances. Then
both laughed. Wilbur's zeal had made him utterly
fearless.

Altogether, Wilbur completed twenty-five glides that day. The longest ones were about two hundred feet.

The next day being Sunday, the brothers rested. In a letter to Chanute, Wilbur wrote:

> I have your letter of Sept. 14th. You can come down at any time most convenient to yourself.
>
> You should bring warm clothing. . . . My brother & I are sleeping on special cots in the second story of our building. We therefore have the two cots which we used last year in reserve for visitors. . . . If you would prefer to sleep aloft as we do, suitable cots can be improvised.

It was now agreed that Orville would begin to pilot the glider. But since it rained on Monday and Dan Tate didn't come to work, the brothers spent much of their time "adjusting the truss wires so as to give an arch to the surfaces." Later, they flew the glider as a kite. "The machine flew beautifully . . . and at times seemed to soar," wrote Orville in his diary.

Both Orville and Wilbur were satisfied.

That Tuesday, Orville climbed into the pilot's space and made several flights. Encouraged by success, it was agreed that after their noon meal, Orville would attempt a long glide from the Big Hill.

After transporting the glider part way up the larger mound, Wilbur had a word of caution. "I think, Orv, that you should make several shallow glides first." He shook his head. "This glider is still tricky."

Orville agreed.

Having managed several shallow hops without difficulty, Orville announced that he was ready for a "real glide."

"Long glides are dangerous," warned Wilbur.

"I know. But I'm ready."

At the top of the hill, Orville crawled into the glider

and signalled that he was ready. His flight continued without mishap for 160 feet.

Wilbur's turn to pilot the craft was next. He stayed aloft for two hundred feet. But as he was flying, he was disturbed by a new problem. The glider suddenly began to sway from side to side in the manner of a garden swing. It did this five or six times. After landing, he and Orville discussed the problem at length. "Perhaps it's the tail," suggested Wilbur.

"I don't know," replied Orville, as he crawled into place.

As the glider mounted into the air, all seemed well. Orville was confident. Then the wings zoomed upward. Alarmed, he twisted "the wing tips to their greatest angle. By this time I found that I was making a descent backwards toward the low wing, from a height of twenty-five or thirty feet," he explained in his diary.

Orville had lost control and the glider began to slip sideways. Wilbur was thoroughly alarmed. Hands funneled to his mouth, he frantically shouted warnings. It was wasted effort. Due to the howling wind, Orville could not hear him; and, even if he had, there was nothing that he could do.

The glider thumped into the hill.

Terrified about his brother's safety, Wilbur ran toward the wreck. But even before he got there, Orville crawled away. Later, Wilbur said, "How he escaped injury I do not know! But afterward he was unable to show a bruise or a scratch anywhere, though his clothes were torn in one place."

Orville was rather calm during and after the whole affair. He wrote in his diary, "The experiments thereupon suddenly came to a close till the repairs can be made. In spite of this sad catastrophe we are tonight in a hilarious mood as a result of the encouraging performance."

One of the reasons the brothers were in "a hilarious mood" was that they had discovered that the glider was *not* ruined beyond repair. True, spars and ribs were cracked, cloth torn, and the right wing tips broken. Nonetheless, they had spare parts. The next morning they took the machine apart and within three or four days they had it back together almost as good as new. As they worked, they discussed the reasons for the wreck.

Both Wilbur and Orville felt assured that their design was correct. The trouble was probably because neither had learned all the secrets of control.

Each evening during the period the repairs were being made, the brothers went for long walks; and, as they walked, they studied the movements of the soaring birds—especially the large ones. These studies led to arguments.

Years later, a man from the lifesaving station

remembered how, as the brothers argued, they swayed their hands and arms as they illustrated what the birds were doing. He wrote, "They would watch the gannets and imitate the movements of the wings of those gannets; we thought they were crazy. But we just had to admire the way they could move their arms this way and that and bend their elbows and wrist bones up and down . . . just like the gannets moved their wings."

The pelican-like gannets, however, were tight-billed with their secrets. Diving for fish to feed their young, the white birds didn't have time to pay much attention to a pair of slender young men who wanted to fly. Wingless humans were beneath their concern!

Shrugging at the birds, Orville and Wilbur were agreed that there was only one way to learn the secret of flight, and that was to continue to experiment.

Life was not dull during the repair and arguing period. Orville's diary for September 27 noted, "At 11 o'clock last night I was awakened by a mouse crawling over my face. Will had advised me that I had better get something to cover my head, or I would have it 'chawed' off. . . . I found on getting up that the little fellow had come to tell me to put another piece of corn bread in the trap. He had disposed of the first piece." This was especially annoying since he had built a "death trap" for his tiny visitor and had "sworn vengeance on the little fellow" for his brazen impudence.

Soon the Wrights were out gliding again. During a two-day period they made about forty glides. As long as they flew straight, they had little trouble. But when they attempted a turn, slight though it might be, they almost always encountered an uncontrollable sliding. This "tailspin," as it is now known, was completely beyond them. Neither could lay a finger on the precise reason.

Harry Combs, in his excellent book, *Kill Devil Hill*, has pointed out the problem they did not understand. "What Orville and Wilbur did not know," he wrote, "is that the fixed vertical fins at the rear of their glider were actually creating trouble instead of curing their problems. When a glider went into a turn, it first had to bank the wings. In the very process of banking, it eased into a sideslip. This caused the vertical fins, which at this point were immovable, *to function as levers*, and this leverage was forcing the wings to rotate about their vertical axis."

In the midst of Orville and Wilbur's experiments, their older brother Lorin dropped in for a fishing vacation. Then George Spratt appeared at the door on October 1.

On October 2, after his guests had all gone to bed, Orville found it hard to get to sleep. All he could think about was the glider's tail. Deep inside, he felt that there should be some way to move it back and forth as they were flying. All of the birds had tails, and all of the birds moved them. But how was this to be done? Could a way be found to arrange a device that would move the tail and warp the wings at the same time? With this thought in mind, he finally dropped into a light sleep.

During breakfast the next morning, Orville caught Lorin's eye, signaling him to watch the drama that was to follow. Then he turned to Wilbur. "Last night," he said, "while I was trying to sleep, I became convinced that we ought to think of a way to twist the tail while we're flying. I think that such a system will solve our problems." He fully expected that Wilbur, in his customary way to show his superiority as an older brother, would say, "Oh, yes, Orv, I was already considering that."

Instead, lost in thought, Wilbur was utterly silent

for a minute or two. Then he said, "I quite agree with you." A little shocked, Orville had to force himself to keep from smiling.

The first change by the Wrights was to remove one of the tail vanes completely. This helped. But the glider kept sliding each time they attempted a turn.

Years later, during a lawsuit in which the Wrights were defending their patents, Wilbur explained, "While this change to make the vane adjustable was being made, the idea came to us of connecting the wires which operated the rudder [tail] to the cables which operated the wing warping, so that whenever the wings were warped the rudder was simultaneously adjusted."

The brothers worked on the changes all day Saturday, October 4. Since the next day was Sunday, they took the day off to rest. During the day, there was a long rain; and, Octave Chanute, along with his assistant, Augustus Herring, moved in with them. They had brought along a multi-winged glider to try out.

On October 6, the smart little mouse was found dead beneath the trunk. The cause of his hoped-for death was unknown.

By October 8 the altered glider was ready. Still cautious, the brothers made twenty glides—all shallow, and straight. The longest was two hundred feet. They continued to practice on the 9th and each flight was excellent. Excited by the new stability, both were anxious for a longer flight. Still, both felt a need for more and more practice.

On the 10th, they transferred to a higher hill. Again, their flight was excellent. "Now, we'll move to the Big Hill," announced Wilbur confidently.

During one long flight, Wilbur turned to the right and then to the left. The response was almost perfect. He was jubilant. But during another glide, the machine suddenly dropped a few feet. Since this only happened once, the brothers were not concerned. (Today, we know they had merely hit an "air pocket.")

Chanute's multi-winged glider made a few pathetic hops. Otherwise, it was a complete failure. The Wrights continued practicing. By the last week of October they had made over one thousand successful flights. Several were over six hundred feet. Wilbur achieved the record by staying aloft twenty-six seconds and covering 622 feet.

Confident they were ready for powered flight, the Wrights stored their glider in the shed. Satisfied that it was safe for the winter, they trudged four miles to Kitty Hawk in the midst of a disheartening drizzle.

On their way to Dayton, the conversation centered on two topics: engines and propellers.

13

The Race Is On

Wilbur was certain that at least one in a dozen companies could build them a suitable lightweight engine; and that since ships had been using propellers for years, he and Orville would find plenty of technical data on how one should be built.

Wilbur was mistaken.

No motor company was even willing to discuss the project, and the Dayton libraries had no information on the construction of propellers. "And so what are you going to do?" asked Kate.

"Simple. We'll build our own engine and design our own propellers!" replied Wilbur without flinching. "Remember Ma used to say, 'Ask, and it shall be given you; seek, and ye shall find; knock, and it shall be opened unto you.' Well, Orv and I have been doing a lot of seeking, asking—and knocking." Remembering their several wrecks he rubbed his head and laughed.

"Oh, Will, you should have been a preacher!"

Later, his hand on the lathe in the back of their

shop, Wilbur faced Charlie Taylor. "We're going to build a motor," he said. "It will have four cylinders, develop at least eight horsepower, run on gasoline, and weigh less than two hundred pounds." He placed his hand on Charlie's shoulder. "And you, Charlie, will do most of the work!"

Taylor stared and his mouth fell slightly ajar. "Me?" he questioned. "I've never built a motor! I did help repair one last year, but that's all." He adjusted his tie. "I'm sorry, I can't help you."

"Nonsense! Orville and I will give you general directions. Our time, of course, will be mostly spent upstairs where we'll be designing the *Flyer*—the new glider we're building to take to Kitty Hawk."

"Do you have a plan?"

"We have a plan for the Flyer, but not for the engine. We'll design it as we put it together."

Taylor's mouth fell even farther ajar. "B-but, Mr. W-Wright," he stammered, "we don't have the proper tools to build an engine."

"We have enough tools," scoffed Wilbur. "We have drills, wrenches, bolts, screwdrivers, and a lathe. If we need any more tools we'll invent them!"

The engine block was cast out of aluminum by a local foundry. With this as a beginning, Charlie went to work. Almost half a century later he remembered:

> We didn't make any drawings. One of us would sketch out the part we were talking about on a piece of scratch paper and I'd spike the sketch over my bench.
>
> It took me six weeks to make that engine.

This engine, copied in part from one used in the old Pope-Toledo car, was an extremely primitive affair. The spark was provided by make-and-break contact points within the combustion chamber. The gas was supplied by an overhead supply and was fed

to the motor by means of gravity. Charlie explained
how the motor worked:

> There was no carburetor as we know it today. The
> fuel was fed into a shallow chamber in the manifold.
> Raw gas blended with air in this chamber, which was
> next to the cylinders.

The first time the engine ran it made such horrible
popping noises that Charlie all but jumped out of his
shoes. While it was bing-banging, rattling the windows, and wallowing in smoke, he exclaimed, "It'll
either explode or throw its flywheel at one of us!"
Since it did neither, he returned from his refuge in
the corner with a bushel basket in front of his chest.

Following a little adjustment, the new engine
behaved slightly better. It, according to a letter written by Orville to George Spratt, had "13 horsepower
on the brake, with a weight of only 150 pounds in the
motor."

In the midst of many heated arguments, the Flyer
gradually came into being. Its wings were slightly over
forty feet long, and the camber was deepened from
one inch in twenty-four inches to one inch in twenty
inches. This would make the flights more difficult to
control; but it would also give more lift, and this was
necessary due to the weight of the motor.

Another change was the gap between the wings.
This was widened from the approximate five feet on
the previous gliders to six feet. The additional space
was to accommodate the motor and the chains that
would turn the propellers.

The Wrights were excited about the progress they
were making on the Flyer, even though their nephew
had dubbed it *The Whopper*. Their next problem was
to design the propellers.

With no tables in existence to indicate the proper

twist for their propellers, the Wrights decided that since the propeller would function something like a wing, they should use the data they had acquired with their wind tunnel. Orville explained their problem and their final solution in his long letter to George Spratt:

> We had been unable to find anything of value in any of the works to which we had access, so we worked out a theory of our own on the subject, and soon discovered, as we usually do, that all the propellers built heretofore are *all wrong*, and then built a pair of propellers 8 1/8 ft. in diameter. . . . Isn't it astonishing that all these secrets have been preserved for so many years just so that we could discover them?

The Wrights filled page after page with calculations in order to decide the precise dimensions of the propellers. This was difficult, for they had to think of the *changing* compression of the air as the propeller moved through it, the *changing* amount of thrust developed, and that of the *changing* vacuum created, and so on. Those variables were exceedingly complicated. Nonetheless, both Orville and Wilbur were confident.

The propellers were carved out of three pieces of spruce carefully glued together. Their main tools were a hatchet and a draw knife. Not being woodworkers by profession, the Wright brothers' success is almost unbelievable. The ends of both propellers were encased in a light duck canvas. This was to keep the wood from splitting. Finally, each propeller was coated with aluminum paint.

Were the propellers properly balanced? They tried them out on a motor in the back of the shop and each propeller met their requirements.

As Orville and Wilbur labored to complete the Flyer, Chanute let them know that Professor Samuel Langley, Secretary of the Smithsonian, was on the

verge of completing a powered aircraft. Doctor
Langley was an important person; and both Wilbur
and Orville held him in high esteem. In 1896 he had
built a thirty-pound aircraft with fourteen-foot wings.
It was powered by two pushing propellers that were
operated by a miniature steam engine. This machine,
launched by a catapult from the roof of a houseboat
on the Potomac, had flown a short distance and then
made a successful landing.

Later, Langley constructed models that flew up to
half a mile.

Inspired by Langley's success, Congress awarded
him fifty thousand dollars with which to build a man-
carrying *Aerodrome*—a name Langley favored for a
flying machine.

"Well, what are you going to do?" asked Kate.

"I guess the race is on," replied Wilbur. "But one
way or another, Orv and I are going to fly!"

"Bravo!" she exclaimed, flashing a confident smile.

As the Wrights perfected their equipment, they remained alert for reports about Samuel Langley and his new Aerodrome. During the second week of August, they learned that Langley had constructed a model one-fourth the size of the Aerodrome. His purpose was to test his theories of balance before he attempted to fly the big one.

Langley launched his model from a catapult on the Potomac on August 8. The experiment was a total failure. The *New York Times* sneered with a headline:

Airship as a Submarine—Defect in Steering Gear Sends it Below the Surface.

The Wrights did not rejoice in the headline. Still, they smiled. There yet remained a chance, perhaps a slight one, to be the first ones to fly in a heavier—than-air machine!

Having dismantled the Flyer and shipped it ahead, the Wrights arrived in Elizabeth City late in the afternoon of September 24. From there they took a steamer to Roanoke Island, and the next morning continued by a gasoline-powered launch to Kitty Hawk.

Dan Tate was with them as they viewed their storage shed. There were huge holes in the building. "We had the worst gales we've ever had," said Tate.

The Wrights were almost breathless as they stepped inside their tattered building. Fortunately, the glider was in good shape. In a letter which Wilbur wrote to Kate on October 1, he said:

> We . . . found everything all right . . . except that a 90-mile wind last February had lifted our building off its foundation and set it over to the east nearly two feet. We made the preparations to begin the erection of the new building on Monday but the conditions for gliding were so fine that we took the machine

out and spent the finest day we have ever had in practice. We made about 75 glides.

These flights were made in the 1902 glider. Both
Orville and Wilbur still believed that their main problem was that of learning to pilot an aircraft. While
they were gliding with the old machine, they began
to assemble the Flyer.

Soon their work was hindered by the rains. In a
long letter addressed to their sister and dated October
18, Wilbur explained:

> The second day opened with the gale still contin-
> uing. . . . We set to work "tooth and nail" (using
> a hammer instead of our teeth however) putting
> braces inside our new building. The climax came
> about 4 o'clock when the wind reached 75 miles an
> hour. Suddenly a corner of our tar-paper roof gave
> way. . . . Orville put on my heavy overcoat, and
> grabbing a ladder sallied forth from the south end
> of the building. . . . He quickly mounted to the edge
> of the roof when the wind caught under his coat and
> folded it back over his head. As the hammer and nails
> were in his pocket and up over his head he was unable
> to get his hands on them or to pull his coattails down,
> so he was compelled to descend again. The next time
> he put the nails in his mouth. . . . He swatted around
> a good little while trying to get a few nails in. . . .
> He explained afterward that the wind kept blowing
> the hammer around so that three licks out of four
> hit the roof or his fingers instead of the nail. . . .
> In the morning we found the larger part of our
> floor was under water. . . .
> According to Dan Tate this storm broke all
> records. . . . Five vessels came ashore between here
> and Cape Henry. . . .
> The "whopper flying machine" is coming on all
> right and will probably be done about Nov. 1st.

About a week after Wilbur mailed this letter, he

received a letter from Chanute saying that he would soon be visiting them. Along with his letter was a news clipping. Wilbur glanced at it casually, then he read it with intense interest. "Look, Orv," he exclaimed, "Langley is about to make another attempt with his Aerodrome!"

Orville studied the clipping. Then, forcing himself to remain calm, he asked, "Do you think he'll be ahead of us?"

"I don't know." Wilbur began to pace back and forth. He snatched the clipping from Orville and read it again. "Time is short," he said, as a hardness came over his face. "Orv, we've got to get busy. It would be terrible to be beaten by a few hours. And remember, Langley has the U.S. Government behind him!"

"What do you propose?"

"Let's put the engine in the Flyer and fly—"

"Before we practice with it as a glider?" Orville shuddered.

"Yes, before we practice with it," answered Wilbur. "It'll be dangerous, but—"

"But don't we need to get the feel of the thing first?"

"We should, but we don't have time. Right now, only two hundred miles to the north, Professor Langley is about to take off. We don't have a choice!"

Heads Or Tails

Early on November 2, Wilbur and Orville began mounting the engine on the lower wing of the Flyer. As they worked, they discovered the nuts for the bolts were missing. Following a little research, the misplaced nuts were found. This problem was a mere taste of problems ahead.

The next day as they were adjusting the warping wires, Dr. George Spratt showed up. His early appearance was a slight irritation, for the Wrights had hoped to be alone for the next few days. Nonetheless, they took advantage of the situation. "We have a sixty-foot rail on which the Flyer will take off," explained one of them. He pointed to four fifteen-foot two-by-fours which had been sheathed on one two-inch side with smooth iron strips. "Why not put them end to end for our first takeoff?"

Spratt carried the sections to a place just west of the shed and placed them end to end. He also made certain that this take-off rail was secure in the sand, was straight, and that it pointed into the direction of a normal wind.

The wind on November 4 was blowing at fifteen miles an hour. Orville and Wilbur were elated. Each was certain that with such perfect weather they couldn't fail.

The one-gallon gasoline tank hanging from a strut was full, the warping system worked, the moving tail responded, and the front elevators were properly set. The motor, likewise, had been properly bolted into place and all the bolts were tight. (One of the chains from the engine to the propeller had been crossed in the form of a figure eight. This was done in order that the blades would whirl in opposite directions, and thus balance one another.)

Before they carried the Flyer over to the launching rail, they started the engine. Since the engine had no exhaust, the explosions were almost deafening. But they were not regular. Wilbur and Orville stared in alarm. It banged, missed, bang-banged, missed-missed, banged. And because of this unevenness, the Flyer shook like a dog shaking off water after a plunge in a lake. Worse, this violent vibration worked many of the screws loose.

Close examination showed that the magneto spark was not large enough to ignite the gasoline; and, worse, the severe shaking had unloosened many screws and damaged both propeller shafts. In addition, the weather had turned extremely cold.

As Orville and Wilbur debated about what they should do, George Spratt announced that he was leaving. He had apparently decided that the Flyer would not take to the air for a long time, if ever. Also, the camp was running out of better-quality food.

The Wrights took advantage of Spratt's leaving by asking him to take the damaged shafts to Norfolk and to mail them, along with a letter of repair instructions to Charlie Taylor in Dayton.

The weather continued to worsen. Amidst the drizzle, Octave Chanute arrived on November 6. Chanute apparently had many doubts about the Wrights ever flying. He felt them out to see if they would be willing to work for him. They weren't.

As the thermometer sank lower and lower, so did the food supply. Groceries ordered from the mainland did not show up. Soon, as Orville wrote to Kate, they were "down to condensed milk and crackers for supper."

Finally, the cold, lack of food, and lack of comforts was too much for the old railroader. Chanute left on the 12th.

Keeping warm was almost impossible. Wilbur described the situation in his now-famous letter to Kate:

> In addition to 1, 2, 3, and 4 blanket nights, we now have 5 blanket nights, & 5 blankets & 2 quilts. Next comes 5 blankets, 2 quilts & fire; then 5, 2, fire & hot water jug. . . . Next comes the addition of sleeping without undressing, then shoes & hat & finally overcoats. . . .

That terrible cold was merely a climax of other weather problems they had endured. Even before Spratt left, Wilbur had explained some of these problems in his note to their sister:

> We found that a fire was absolutely necessary. . . . We took one of the carbide cans and, after punching some holes in the bottom for air, built a fire in it. . . . Of course the smoke was so intense there was no standing up in the room, so we sat down on the floor around the can with tears streaming down our cheeks. . . . Everything about the building was sooted up so thoroughly that for several days we couldn't sit down to eat without a whole lot of black soot dropping down in our plates.

That problem, however, was modified, for they finally put up "a stove pipe and built a stove out of a can." Nonetheless, when they awakened on Thursday, they found the water in their basin had frozen.

During those shivering days, as they awaited the arrival of the shafts, they kept busy tightening screws and making other adjustments. They also got their magneto to producing healthy sparks.

Now, if only those shafts would come!

The shafts arrived on the 20th and the Wrights were pleased with the repairs Taylor had made. "You did a most excellent job," wrote Orville.

Wilbur and Orville had just installed the shafts when they faced another difficulty. In spite of everything they tried, they could not make the sprocket plates attached to the shafts remain in place. Utterly baffled, Orville closed his diary with his most pessimistic line, "Day closes in deep gloom."

The next day, however, they conceived the idea of keeping the sprockets tight by loading their threads with Arnstein's tire cement. The miracle adhesive worked! "We can now adjust the engine," said Wilbur, wrench in hand.

The engine shook and jerked just as before. Calm examination revealed the trouble was in the fuel line. The cure was simple. They fixed the valve so that vibrations could neither open nor close it. The engine now ran smoothly. One cylinder, however, seldom worked.

Wilbur and Orville consulted together and experimented. Soon the engine was purring like a kitten. Always careful, they spent the next three days tuning, adjusting, making ready. On the afternoon of the 25th they were ready to fly. The motor was behaving beautifully.

Then the clouds began to drizzle.

The rain, slight though it was, would drench the fabric in the Flyer's wings, and this additional weight would keep it on the ground. They had no alternative but to wait.

As the brothers waited for clear weather, their minds kept wandering two hundred miles north to the Potomac. Each one secretly thought about Professor Langley. *Had his Aerodrome been able to fly? If so, how long did it remain in the air?*

The weather showed no signs of clearing. The drizzle was followed by snow. Then on the 28th, Wilbur had good news. "There's a possibility that we may have a clear day," he said. Orville studied the sky. Yes, there were positive signs!

While they waited for the sun to break through, they examined the Flyer again. Yes, the tail responded. Yes, the wings warped. Yes, the elevators moved in response to the cradle. Yes, the chains to the propellers were in good shape. Then a hollow place suddenly formed in Wilbur's stomach. After running the motor for about three minutes, he discovered a long hairline crack in one of the propeller shafts. "Just look at that, Orv!" he exclaimed.

Orville studied it. "The crack goes the whole length of the shaft," he said grimly. "What will we do?" He rubbed his moustache.

Wilbur shook his head. "We can't fly it this way. If we do, everything could be shaken to pieces. That shaft won't last."

"Then, what shall we do?"

"You, Orv, will have to take the shafts back to Dayton and build new ones. This time, make them out of solid spring steel!"

Orville left for Dayton on Monday, November 30.

Wilbur tried to make use of his time while he waited. He studied the Flyer, recalculated their charts,

paced the floor, hoped—and prayed. Winter was setting in. New storms were brewing. One evening as
he was pacing the floor, Wilbur remembered the time
he had faced Orville on the train as they were returning to Dayton. At that time he had said, "You know,
Orv, men will not fly in our lifetime. No, they will
not fly in a thousand years!"

Now, he wondered, *Was I right? Are we just wasting
our money? Maybe the people were correct who scoffed at them
and said that if God had wanted men to fly He would have
given them wings.*

A few weeks before this, Dr. Simon Newcomb had
published an article in the *Independent* which showed
by clear logic that it was utterly impossible for men
to fly. The Wrights at this time had probably not seen
that article, but in their dark moments both were
tempted to come to the same conclusion.

Early one morning, just before dawn, Wilbur's
mind went back to his mother's bedside just before
her death. Her thin fingers holding his hand, she had
whispered in her deep yet low voice, "Son, always
remember Paul's words in Romans 8:28, 'And we
know that all things work together for good to them
that love God.' " Again and again those words had
proven to be true in his life. Undoubtedly it was the
providence of God that had led him to discover the
hairline crack in the propeller shaft. Otherwise! . . .
He shuddered as he considered the possibilities that
might have followed if that shaft had completely
cracked during an attempted flight.

Strengthened by his meditation, he got out of bed
and shaved. While he adjusted the new tie Kate had
given him, a fresh resolve came over him. The fact
that Chanute and Spratt had given up on him meant
nothing. Both he and Orville were going to fly!

Orville returned with the new shafts on December

11. He had also brought along a news clipping about Langley and his Aerodrome. The story told how Langley had launched his huge machine on December 8. *The New York Times* reported: "On the signal to start, the aeroplane glided smoothly along the launching tramway, until the end of the slide was reached. Then, left to itself, the aeroplane broke in two and turned completely over."

Manly, the pilot, was rescued by another assistant who, fully clothed, leaped into the Potomac and pulled him out. The headline in the *Washington Post* was almost nasty. It read: "Buzzard a Wreck."

"I'm glad the pilot was rescued," said Wilbur. "Now, let's get to work!"

By the 12th, the Flyer was ready to be flown.

On Sunday, the 13th, the weather was perfect; and the fifteen-mile-an-hour wind was just right. Nonetheless, it was the Lord's Day! While Wilbur and Orville rested, Mr. Etheridge of the Kitty Hawk Life Saving Station brought his wife and children over to have a look at the Flyer.

The skies on Monday, the 14th, were fair. But the morning wind was a mere five-miles-an-hour. While they waited for it to increase, they worked on the Flyer's tail. Since their lives might depend on it, the tail had to be just right. Determined that their first flight should be witnessed, the Wrights had made an agreement with the men at the Life Saving Station. "When we're ready to fly, we'll hoist our flag and we hope that all of you will come."

Since the wind had not increased sufficiently to take off from a flat place, the brothers decided to make their attempt from the Big Hill. There, the slope would help them. At 1:30 P.M. they pulled their flag to the top of the post. Now that the weight of the motor had increased the total weight of the Flyer to six hundred

pounds, moving the machine to the Big Hill was quite
a task. They solved the problem by placing the Flyer
on the takeoff rail, pushing it to the end, and then
moving the back pieces of the rail up front. It was hard
work, but with the help of Robert Wescott, W.S.
Dough, ''Uncle Benny'' O'Neal, John T. Daniels,
and Thomas Beacham from the Life Saving Station,
they made the move in less than three-quarters of an
hour.

The takeoff rail—Junction Railroad, Wilbur called
it—was placed about 150 feet up the slope, which
slanted downward at about an eight-degree angle.
While they were working, a couple of small boys and
their dog, who had accompanied the men from Kitty
Hawk, stood nearby and watched every move.

They watched as a ''launching dolly'' with two
wheels made from bicycle hubs equipped with ball
bearings was placed on the takeoff rail. Wilbur and
Orville moved it back and forth to make certain there
was no drag. Next, a long wire was attached to the
dolly and secured on the hill. (The purpose of this was
to hold the Flyer secure until the pilot signaled he was
ready to take off.)

Finally, the Flyer was mounted on the dolly.

The next problem was to decide who would go first.
At about three o'clock, Wilbur tossed a coin. Orville
announced his choice. Wilbur won. Wilbur crawled
onto the lower wing and secured his hips in the cradle.
Moments later, the engine was started. The sound
was too much for the boys and the dog. They
scampered away in full flight and hid behind a hill.

Orville held the tip of one wing and one of the
visitors held the other. Wilbur studied the situation
as he was lying down in the pilot's position. Then he
shouted, ''I'm ready,'' and pulled the wire. But it
wouldn't release. The wire was too taut as the Flyer

strained to go forward. Orville then shouted for some men to pull the machine back a trifle. When this was done, the wire was released and the Flyer began to rush down the takeoff rail. As it moved forward, Orville ran alongside and held the wing tip in order to keep it properly balanced.

At the end of ten yards, Orville was out of breath.

Nearly six feet from the end of the rail, the Flyer rose sharply into the air. Orville snapped his stopwatch, and held his breath. The Flyer reached a height of about fifteen feet. Eyes glued onto the whirling blades, Orville assumed that Wilbur would continue on to Kitty Hawk. But Wilbur was having trouble. Slowly the machine sank until it was just above the ground. Then it straightened out. Wilbur's hopes soared. But the left wing was too low. It caught in the sand and whirled the Flyer around. Quickly Wilbur turned the gas off.

The engine had made 602 revolutions. The Flyer had remained in the air three and a half seconds and covered 105 feet from the end of the takeoff rail.

Other than a cracked skid and a crumpled elevator, the damage was slight. Wilbur was not hurt.

In a letter to the family, Wilbur explained what happened:

> We took to the hill and after tossing for first whack, which I won, got ready for the start. The wind was a little to one side and the track was not exactly straight downhill. . . . However the real trouble was an error of judgment, in turning up too suddenly after leaving the track. . . . The machinery all worked together in entirely satisfactory manner. . . .There is now no question of final success.

Neither Wilbur nor Orville believed that they had made a successful flight. To them, Wilbur had merely made a short glide. A real flight would have to be made from level ground.

Wilbur and Orville spent December 15 and 16 making repairs. They hoped to fly on the 17th. But that Thursday morning winds of twenty-four to thirty miles an hour were blowing fine sand through the air beneath a darkening sky. Puddles of frozen water stood about the camp. Other than for a number of courageous gulls, the sky was almost empty of birds.

As the brothers warmed their hands at a fire, the anemometer pointed to an almost twenty-seven-mile-an-hour wind. Both Wilbur and Orville knew they would be risking their lives to fly into such a gust. But perhaps it would slacken off within an hour or two. At 10:00 A.M. they ran their flag up. Then they began to lay their takeoff rail.

Soon John T. Daniels, W.S. Dough, A.D. Etheridge, W.C. Brinkley, and Johnny Moore—a seventeen-year-old from Nags Head—showed up. All of them were encased in their overcoats. While the five shivering observers stood around, Orville placed his camera on a tripod and focused it so that the picture would show the Flyer just as it lifted from the track. He then turned to John Daniels. "Come over here and trip the camera at the exact moment of liftoff."

Daniels asked for some detailed instructions, and then he stood waiting for the right moment to snap the important picture.

At exactly 10:35 Orville adjusted his hips in the cradle. The engine had been warming up and the anemometer indicated a still dangerous twenty-miles-an-hour wind. (Unknown to them, the anemometer at Kitty Hawk was registering twenty-seven miles an hour!)

As Orville prepared to release the wire, Wilbur faced the crowd, "Don't look sad," he exhorted, "laugh and holler . . . clap . . . and try to cheer Orville," or so Daniels remembered.

Orville released the wire and the Flyer was on its way. Liftoff occurred at the beginning of the fourth rail. The machine reached a height of ten feet and continued in an up-and-down manner. The flight covered a distance of 120 feet and lasted *about* twelve seconds. The Wrights were never quite sure that the stopwatch had been turned off at the right moment.

Repairs to a skid, cracked in landing, having been made, the Flyer was returned to the starting place on the takeoff rail. It was now Wilbur's turn. He released the wire at 11:20. His flight was similar to that of Orville's—complete with the up-and-down movements. However, he managed to remain in the air for an extra second and to cover an additional fifty feet. Also, he landed without mishap.

Orville took off at 11:40. He remembered: "When out about the same distance as Will's, I met with a strong gust from the left which raised the left wing and sidled the machine off to the right in a lively manner. I immediately turned the rudder to bring the machine down."

This time the Flyer remained in the air for fifteen seconds and flew two hundred feet.

The brothers were making progress!

Wilbur crawled into position at twelve o'clock. In a moment he was in the cradle. Then he was in the air. The Flyer moved up and down. Soon it passed the two hundred foot mark. Next, three hundred. At this point Wilbur had better control. The flight smoothed. On, on it went. It passed four hundred feet, then five hundred, six hundred, seven hundred.

Still it continued. Orville's eyes widened as the wings and whirling propellers grew smaller. At about

eight hundred feet Wilbur tried to go a trifle higher to miss a sandy ridge. Then the Flyer began to pitch. Wilbur tried desperately to regain control. It was wasted effort. The first heavier-than-air machine to carry a man touched sand. Its skids dug deep. The Flyer was thrown forward and its elevator was twisted out of line. Nonetheless, Wilbur had flown 852 feet and had remained in the air fifty-nine seconds.

Two BKs had achieved what some Ph.D.'s said was impossible.

Stunned by success, Wilbur stood alone and stared. Three minutes later Orville and a few others were at his side. As they were congratulating him and making plans to repair the Flyer for Orville's turn, a gust of wind lifted it by the front and smacked it down. Orville and Daniels rushed to protect it. They were too late. The machine turned over and over like a giant tumbleweed. Orville jumped clear. Daniels wasn't so fortunate. Again and again he was slammed against the chains and motor. He remembered: "When the thing did stop for a second I nearly broke up every wire and upright getting out of it."

Other than for a few bruises, scratches, and torn clothes, Daniels emerged in good condition. But the Flyer had been completely wrecked. Still, it had served a purpose.

Shivering with cold, Orville and Wilbur returned to their quarters. They lunched, washed dishes, rested, and set out for Kitty Hawk—four miles away. The brisk walk helped keep them warm.

Since there was no telegraph office at Kitty Hawk, the Weather Station was permitted to send messages to Norfolk where they were relayed. After entering the warm building, Orville composed a wire:

SUCCESS FOUR FLIGHTS THURSDAY MORNING
ALL AGAINST TWENTY-ONE-MILE WIND STARTED

FROM LEVEL WITH ENGINE POWER ALONE AVERAGE
SPEED THROUGH AIR THIRTY-ONE MILES LONGEST
59 SECONDS INFORM PRESS HOME CHRISTMAS.
                              ORVILLE WRIGHT.

Orville handed the message to Joseph Dosher. Having sent it, Dosher had a question. "The Norfolk man wants to know if it's all right to give the story to a reporter friend."

The Wrights answered immediately: "No!" (They refused because they had agreed the news of the breakthrough should reach the world by way of Dayton.) But the Norfolk operator couldn't resist. He passed the message to H. P. Moore of the *Virginian-Pilot*. Moore queried twenty-one newspapers if they wanted the story. Five of them did. But only three used it the following morning.

Since the *Virginian-Pilot* was a member of the AP, that news-gathering agency had access to the story. They chose not to use it at that time. (It probably sounded too unbelievable!)

After packing their dismantled plane, Wilbur and Orville headed for Dayton.

15

Ignored

By the time the Wrights stepped off the train in Dayton on December 23 they were utterly sick of the fantastic stories that had been printed about them.

While waiting in Norfolk, Wilbur showed Orville the headline in the *Virginian-Pilot*. It declared that they had "flown for 3 miles in the teeth of a high wind." And a few paragraphs later it stated that there had been a six-bladed propeller beneath the machine "for lift." Also it stated that Orville had run around shouting, "Eureka!"

Because of this story and others, the Wrights practically ignored the newsmen who confronted them as they stepped into their home on Hawthorn Street. For them, the Christmas season was marred by the untruthful stories that had been printed. As they were relaxing in the living room, Bishop Wright showed them a clipping from the Dayton *Daily News*. In a tiny inside headline near the country correspondence section, it stated: "Dayton Boys Emulate Great Santos-Dumont."

Wilbur almost glared. "Santos-Dumont has only
flown in balloons! Don't the editors know that there
is a vast difference between lighter-than-air and
heavier-than-air flying machines?" he demanded, his
eyes shooting fire.

The Wrights had accomplished several firsts and
had applied for patents. But their parents had drilled
into them that they should constantly search for truth.
"Ye shall know the truth and the truth shall make
you free," thundered their father. Fifty-nine seconds
in the air was a sensational breakthrough. Still—

Since their gliding days were over, there was no
need to return to Kitty Hawk. Now, their great need
was access to space—and privacy.

Torrence Huffman, president of Dayton's Fourth
National Bank, offered them free use of his farm,
Huffman Prairie, eight miles east of the city limits.
Since it was near Simms Station, a connection of the
interurban trolley, and was screened on two sides with
forty and fifty-foot-high trees, it was ideal. The bank
president's only requirement was that they not disturb
his cattle.

Within days, Orville and Wilbur were designing
Wright Flyer II. Since they would be depending on the
motor for lift, the wing camber was lowered from one
in twenty inches to one in twenty-five inches. This
meant that the control would be less sensitive. The
new machine weighed eight hundred pounds and its
engine was enlarged so as to deliver about fifteen to
sixteen horsepower. The brothers were confident they
would set new records. But they had an immediate
problem to overcome.

At Kitty Hawk the takeoff rail could be laid perfectly
straight in the sand. But flat though it was, Huffman
Prairie was punctuated with six-inch-high hummocks.

Being careful, however, they managed to lay sixty feet of takeoff rail in spite of these "warts."

But sixty feet was not enough. Due to the higher altitude and the more shallow wings, Wright Flyer just would not lift into the air. (Kitty Hawk was at sea level while Huffman Prairie was 815 feet.) The obvious solution was to lengthen the takeoff rail so that the machine could gain more speed. They lengthened it to one hundred and sixty feet.

Confident that Wright Flyer II would lift into the air, the brothers invited the press to witness their attempt of May 25, 1904. About fifty people showed up, including a dozen reporters. That afternoon, while reporters held their pencils ready, the Wrights reported that since the wind was blowing too hard there would be a delay. As the crowd waited, the machine was eased back to its shed.

After an hour of waiting, a slight rain began to fall. This meant another hour's wait. Finally, the Wrights were ready. Eagerly the reporters began to take notes. The Flyer was brought out and the motor started. Wilbur climbed inside, adjusted his hips in the cradle, pulled the wire, and was off. The machine whizzed down the rail, but instead of rising into the air, it merely slipped into the grass.

"I'm sorry," explained Wilbur. "We're having trouble with the motor. Come back tomorrow."

The next day the number of reporters had decreased. This time the would-be flying-machine rose about seven or eight feet in the air, glided sixty feet, and then slid to the ground. Two pieces of the landing skids were cracked.

The disappointed newsmen turned in their stories. Most of them simply explained that problems had developed. These articles plus the fact that they were reprinted in many other papers kept the crowds away.

This pleased the Wrights, for they liked to work in privacy.

During their first dozen tries, Wright Flyer II only managed one decent flight. But the brothers were not discouraged. They now left the bicycle business up to the management of Charlie Taylor and concentrated on flying. Soon it occurred to them that their main problem was taking off from the rail. Due to the hummocks they couldn't lay a takeoff rail long enough. They solved this problem by building a catapult to give the machine an extra shove.

The catapult consisted of a sixteen hundred pound weight that fell sixteen and a half feet to the ground. This weight was attached by pulleys and ropes to the machine. With this apparatus, Flyer II was frequently in the air after a run of only fifty feet.

Nonetheless, it wasn't until they had made fifty-one flights that they broke their Kitty Hawk record of fifty-nine seconds, and then did so by only one second! However, they were learning to fly; and before the year was out, they had managed two five-minute flights. Better yet, during those flights they had circled the field on each occasion from four to five times.

This was progress!

Strangely, even though passengers on the interurban trolley occasionally saw their machine in the air, they were not impressed. They reasoned: If those derby-hatted boys are really flying, the newspapers would mention it. But since the papers were silent, they merely shrugged. Indeed, one day as Wilbur and Orville were heading toward Simms Station, they heard a burly man exclaim angrily, ''That would be as impossible as it would be for a man to fly!''

During all of 1904, the Wrights had kept Flyer II in the air for only forty-five minutes. Nonetheless, they were confident that soon they would be able to remain in the air for an hour or more during a single flight.

While the newspapers were ignoring them in 1905, the Wrights continued to make improvements. They widened the propellers, increased the power of the motor, enlarged the tail and the elevators—and placed them farther from the wings. In addition, they made the struts much stronger. (Later, British historians referred to this machine as "the first practical airplane in the world.")

On the improved machine's first flight August 24, Orville covered a total of 1556 feet in just less than 32 seconds. On the same day, Wilbur flew 2300 feet. Four days later he went 2775 feet, and a little later in the same day he stayed aloft for 79 seconds and made 4257 feet.

"Do you think you'll ever fly an entire mile?" asked their father.

"Of course," replied Wilbur. "Just give us time!"

On September 6, Orville's first flight lasted for only forty seconds and covered merely two thousand feet. But he tried again. This time, Wilbur could hardly believe what he was seeing. The improved Wright Flyer II kept going around and around the field. It stayed aloft for an entire minute, then two minutes, then three, then four. Then, just six seconds short of five minutes, it landed where it had started.

"How far did I go?" asked Orville.

"Fifteen thousand six hundred and nine feet!" almost shouted Wilbur.

"That's nearly three miles." Orville shook his head.

"Right. You only lacked 231 feet."

On September 26, Wilbur flew eleven miles and was aloft for eighteen minutes. Better yet, he only landed because he was out of gas. Then on October 3, Orville exceeded fifteen miles. Two days later,

Wilbur topped that record by remaining above ground for thirty-nine minutes and twenty-three seconds. Moreover, he whizzed through the air at the breathless speed of thirty-eight miles an hour and flew 24.2 miles.

Their success caused a problem. Lying in the machine for such long periods was hard on their necks. At the end of Wilbur's longest flight, his neck was so stiff he could barely twist it. Heads together, the brothers designed a new model. Now the pilot—and passenger—could sit upright!

While all this progress was being made, the newspapers continued to ignore them. (Years later, Dan Kumler, former editor of Dayton's *Daily News* was asked the reason for his silence. "We didn't believe the stories we heard," he confessed with a warm smile and shrug.)

The question in a popular joke was: "When will men fly?" The answer: "When the laws of gravity are repealed!"

Sunday school teacher, Amos I. Root, of Medina, Ohio, however, was at least a mild believer. Facing his Sunday school class, this dealer in honey and publisher of *Gleanings in Bee Culture*, had an edge-of-the-seat story.

"There are two Ohio men who have outstripped the world in demonstrating that a flying-machine can be constructed without the aid of a balloon." He read a short note about the Wrights from a clipping he had cut from an Akron paper. He then added, "When they make their next trial, I'm going to try and be on hand." He used the word *try* because Dayton was 175 miles away—a long journey in those days.

Thoroughly enjoying their privacy, Wilbur and Orville continued to experiment. But each additional success made them even more wary of spies; for, although the general public scoffed at their work, others, like Glenn Curtis, were trying to develop a machine that could be sold to the government.

One day two visitors got off the trolley at Simms Station and walked over to Huffman's Prairie. "Is it all right to look around?" asked one of them.

"Certainly," replied one of the brothers. "Only we'd rather that you didn't take pictures."

The man hesitated. Then he laid his camera down about twenty feet away. Returning, he asked, "May I look around in the shed?"

The brother was suspicious. "Are you a newspaperman?"

"No, but I do some writing."

After he had looked around and left, Charlie Taylor commented, "That man's no writer. When he looked at the different parts of the machine he called them all by their right names."

Thoroughly alarmed, Wilbur and Orville

exchanged glances. From that time on, they were more secretive than ever.

Having observed a short flight, Amos I. Root published a long article about the Wrights— "minister's boys who love machinery"—in *Gleanings in Bee Culture*. (This article was the first article by an eyewitness of powered flight.) Root was enthusiastic. "When Columbus discovered America he did not know what the outcome would be. No one living can give a guess of what is coming. Possibly we may fly over the north pole."

After the article was published, Root sent a marked copy to the *Scientific American*, hoping they would reprint it.

The *Scientific American* wasn't interested.

Those who talked about heavier-than-air flying-machines were still using such words as: delusion, humbug, impossible, crackpot, fraud.

Toward the end of October, 1906, Orville and Wilbur read in the papers that Alberto Dantos-Dumont, a wealthy Brazilian living in Paris, had actually flown. The Wrights were not impressed when it was reported that he had flown over Paris and around the Eiffel Tower, for he had accomplished this using a lighter-than-air gas bag. And, although his October flight had been in a heavier-than-air machine called the *14-bis*, it had flown merely two hundred feet.

As Wilbur read how the crowds had cheered at this achievement, he sniffed, "He didn't fly. He only made a hop. We did better than that three years ago!"

About a month later, however, Santos-Dumont flew for 720 feet. This time the crowds went wild. Men shouted. Women cried. Some fainted. The European press exploded with acclaim. Headlines screamed that Santos-Dumont was the first to fly.

The Wrights read the reports and were silent. The

world was acclaiming a man who had flown only 720 feet when they had flown over 24 miles in one flight. Rightful acclaim, and contracts for production, really belonged to them!

While the world acclaimed Santos-Dumont, several groups approached the Wrights. "Why don't you make a public demonstration of your flying-machine?"

"It already flies. We're waiting for solid offers to buy the Flyer. And while we're waiting, we don't want anyone to steal our secrets," replied the Wrights.

"How about a semi-public showing of your machine?" asked another group.

"No."

"How about flying before a strictly private committee," requested others.

"No."

"Why not?"

"Because we are securing patents and we do not want any close-up photographs taken."

Charles Flint, a wealthy industrialist, now tried to make a deal with the Wrights. Convinced that they should make a public showing of the Flyer, he had a representative outline a sensational idea. In April, 1907, there would be a grand celebration of the three hundredth anniversary of the founding of Jamestown, Virginia. All sorts of celebrities would be there, including President Theodore Roosevelt. Many battleships would also be present.

In the midst of this celebration, the Wrights could take off from Kitty Hawk, circle the battleships, and land in Albemarle Sound.

The Wrights were interested. But there were problems. How could they keep spies from taking photographs? The answer was that the entire machine could be painted silver. This would produce such a glare in any photograph that secret details could not be seen.

The next problem was even more difficult. How would they land? If they landed at Albemarle Sound they would need pontoons. Could they get them in time?

They tried. It was impossible.

Finally the entire idea was dropped.

Day after day the Wrights waited for someone to make them a substantial offer for their invention. No one did. Utterly ignored by everyone but cranks, they felt as popular as a porcupine in a balloon factory. Then on May 15, a telegram came from Flint's office urging them to go to Europe. Perhaps someone in Paris or Berlin or London would be interested in their invention.

"How about it?" asked Orville, fingering the yellow telegram.

"I'm on my way," replied Wilbur. He packed one suitcase and stepped out the door. He sailed from New York City for Liverpool on the *Campania*. The date was May 18, 1907.

16

Success

Excited about the success of Santos-Dumont and others, the Europeans were rather unconcerned about the secretive Wrights and their flying-machine. Santos-Dumont was their man! Wilbur felt the chill of indifference the moment he landed. In a letter mailed from London on May 25, he wrote:

We reached Liverpool at about 7 A.M. today and London at 12:30 by the special train. Mr. Berg met me and took me to the Morley's National Hotel opposite the Nelson Monument in Trafalgar Square. . . . I noticed the dome of St. Paul's just behind us. . . . I have had only about fifteen minutes to look around as I've been talking to Mr. Berg.

Berg is fully convinced that there is little hope of doing business with England or the French Government in the near future.

In Germany Loewe is afraid to do anything toward bringing it to the personal attention of the Emperor.

I ordered a dress suit today for 7 pounds and a dinner jacket for 4 pounds. They are the best the tailor had and I think would cost close to a hundred dollars at home.

(P.S.) It is not our intention for the present to let it be known that I am in Europe, except to a very few.

Although sale prospects looked discouraging, Wilbur had made up his mind to enjoy Europe. When F.R. Cordley, a member of the Flint firm, invited him and Berg to accompany him on a vacation to Paris, Wilbur was ready to go. He had endured mosquitoes, teeth-chattering nights, crashes, and other disasters before. With Romans 8:28 as a motto, he was a patient man.

The weather in Paris was perfect and France seemed to have a flower in her hair. He visited the Place de la Concorde where Marie Antoinette was executed, strolled down the Avenue des Champs Elysées to the Arc de Triomphe, and took his first ride in a balloon. But even while he was enjoying the magnificent horse chestnut trees, his mind was on reaching a satisfactory agreement with someone for his and Orville's invention.

Within a few days there were several nibbles. But each offer required a demonstration. There was only one solution. Orville had to disassemble, crate, ship the Flyer, and sail for Europe.

Orville arrived in Paris on Sunday, July 28.

Bargaining between the brothers and the French Government continued. No progress was made. Then a high official suggested that if the Wrights added $50,000 to their price and turned the money over to him, things would go smoother. Both Wilbur and Orville shuddered at such an idea. Neither believed in bribes. But Wilbur had an idea. ''We'll agree provided you mention the charge in the contract and make a notation that it is for your services.''

That was the end of that deal!

Stalling and excuses followed.

On November 5 Léon Delagrange flew fifteen hundred feet. This success created a sensation and European newspapers headlined the story. Then it was announced that Henri Farman, son of a British journalist, would make a public flight near Paris on November 9. Wilbur attended the demonstration.

Farman's machine was even more primitive than the Kitty Hawk machine of 1903. With his derby sitting squarely on his head, Wilbur watched. Farman's machine lifted into the air, flew half a mile and then landed. The flight lasted thirty seconds. The crowd was hysterical. The people shouted, waved flags, wept, boasted, stamped their feet. Some even screamed.

The French newspapers flamed with more headlines. One of them blazed: "It was the most wonderful flight ever made in such a contrivance."

Knowing that he had flown twenty-four miles, Wilbur had to force himself to keep smiling. His patience had finally run out. He sailed for New York City on November 11.

Orville remained in France, for he and Wilbur had ordered a pair of spare motors to be built by Barriquand and Marre—a firm in Paris. Shortly after these motors were completed, Orville returned to Dayton. The Flyer remained in the warehouse at Le Havre.

Unexpectedly, Delagrange and Farman's flights had stirred America. They had proved to a yawning public that had all but ignored the bishop's sons that human flight in heavier-than-air machines was possible. Now Washington was ready with a "contract." This contract bristled with ifs.

One *if* stipulated that the Wright Flyer had to fly at a demonstration during the next September. Another that the machine had to average forty miles an hour. (Speed was very important. If the Flyer's speed was less than thirty-six miles an hour, the contract would be cancelled. But for every single mile it averaged above forty miles an hour, they would receive an extra twenty-five hundred dollars.

If the Flyer passed the test at forty miles an hour, the Wrights would receive twenty-five thousand dollars.

Bishop Milton Wright noted in his diary for February 8, 1908, that his sons had signed this contract—and that it had been accepted. This agreement stipulated that the new aircraft would carry two men.

The Wrights set aside two hundred days in which to build their machine for this test. Since they had decided that it would have to weigh between 1,100 and 1,250 pounds they would have to improve their engine, even though it was already producing thirty-five horsepower. Also, they would have to develop the seating arrangement and new guiding levers.

"Will you get it done in time?" asked their father.

"Of course!" replied each of them.

The bishop smiled and rumbled inside.

Three weeks after their agreement with the United States Government, the Wrights received a contract from France. This contract agreed to pay them one hundred thousand dollars cash if their machine passed a public test the next fall.

Turning to Orville, Wilbur exulted, "We'll be flying on both continents at about the same time, and that suits me fine! You can fly the machine we're now building. I'll fly the one in the crates at Le Havre."

As the brothers worked on their new machine, they made arrangements to fly it at Kitty Hawk. Since time was short, no day seemed quite long enough. "I wish there were eight days in a week," muttered Orville.

The calendar urged them on. And so did the newspapers. On May 21 a headline reported that Glenn Curtiss had flown more than a thousand feet, and that he had made quarter turns to both the left and the right.

A few days later, on May 30, Léon Delagrange remained in the air for a quarter of an hour and covered seven miles. Then, a mere three weeks later, Glenn Curtiss flew half a mile twice; and, on July 4th had celebrated Independence Day by remaining above ground for almost two minutes.

Next, two days after Delagrange's success, Louis Blériot took off in a single-winged machine and set a record for speed. He flew six miles in eight minutes! His achievement, however, was overshadowed by Henry Farman; for, on the same day, Farman circled around for twenty minutes.

"The race continues!" remarked Wilbur one day as he wearily slipped into bed. "But I have a feeling that we're still out front."

The Wrights barred all reporters from their activities at Kitty Hawk. Nonetheless, the reporters slipped up on them and watched their doings through powerful telescopes.

On May 7, the *Times* had a one-page headline:

The Wrights Fly 1,000 Feet.

Two days later, the same paper announced that the brothers had completed ten flights.

The Wrights were unhappy about this publicity. Yet they didn't have time to worry. Competition was crowding them. They had to make adjustments in order to coax the last ounce of performance out of their machine. Also, they had to have two men in the air at the same time!

On May 14, Wilbur and Charles Furnas, a Dayton mechanic who worked for the Wrights, nervously took their seats. The machine lifted into the air and flew six hundred feet. Then it went up again. From a distance, a newspaperman was watching. A day later, his readers picked up their papers and read:

> There was something weird, almost uncanny, about the whole thing. Here on this lonely beach was being performed the greatest act of the ages, but there were no spectators and no applause save the booming of the surf and the startled cries of the sea birds. . . . Flocks of gulls and crows, screaming and chattering, darted and circled about the machine.

But that reporter did not get the full story. Unknown to him, while Wilbur circled out of his sight behind a sand dune, the machine was suddenly tossed about by a sudden gust of wind. Momentarily confused, Wilbur pushed the wrong lever. The machine crashed to the ground, plowed into the sand, and smashed the elevators. Otherwise, neither he nor his passenger were seriously hurt.

Realizing that the crash was merely because of a mistake, neither brother was alarmed. They always learned by their mistakes! Both were confident that Orville would pass the United States Government's tests that fall.

As Wilbur headed for France, his deepest concern was that his younger brother would succeed. Orville was not as thorough as he was. And yet— Wilbur was confident that the Flyer would do well.

Alas, Wilbur knew nothing of the troubles ahead!

Wilbur landed at LeHavre on Friday, May 29, and reached Paris the same day. He soon learned that Berg was a trifle discouraged. Also, the French newspapers began to attack both him and Orville. They saw no point in allowing the Wrights to test their machine since French machines were already vastly superior to theirs.

Fortunately for Wilbur, he could not read French.

Ignoring the hostile atmosphere, Wilbur went to the firm of Bariquand and Marre to inspect the motors he and Orville had ordered. Neither was satisfactory. He ordered changes and left a design for the fan. They promised that the motors would be ready for trial within a week.

On June 8, Wilbur boarded a train in Paris and headed for Le Mans, a small city about one hundred miles southwest of Paris. On a race course just outside the city, Léon Bollée, an automobile manufacturer, had suggested that Wilbur make his trial flights. Since the race course seemed ideal, and Monsieur Bollée had offered him a large room in which to reassemble the Flyer, Wilbur agreed at once.

The crated Flyer was shipped to Le Mans immediately. But when Wilbur opened those crates he was shocked. In a letter to Orville, dated June 17, Wilbur wrote:

> I opened the boxes yesterday and have been puzzled ever since to know how you could have wasted two full days packing them. I am sure that with a scoop shovel I could have put things in within two or three minutes and made as fully as good a job of it. I never saw such evidences of idiocy in my life. . . . Ten or a dozen ribs were broken. . . . The cloth is torn in almost numberless places. . . . The radiators are badly mashed; the seat is broken; the magneto has the oil cap broken off, the coils are torn up, and I suspect the axle is bent a little.''

He also had other complaints. There were no nuts on the bolts. Numerous bolts were lost. Many of the bolts had not been replaced in their proper holes. But since complaining didn't help, Wilbur adjusted his tie and went to work. He still had confidence in Romans 8:28!

Along with a crew of French workers, Wilbur put in a minimum of ten hours a day. And as the Flyer came together, his confidence began to grow. Then, on Saturday, July 4, he had an accident. While testing one of the motors, he had it turning at fifteen hundred rpm when suddenly the radiator hose came loose. At the time, he was standing with his sleeves rolled up only a foot away. The furiously boiling water struck him full blast on the left arm and chest.

Fortunately Monsieur Bollée was nearby at the time and eased him to the floor. Also, he had some picric acid on hand. This he smeared over Wilbur's arm and chest. In a letter to his father, written five days later, Wilbur wrote: "My forearm was bare and suffered the worst, though the scald over my heart had more dangerous possibilities. . . . The blister on my arm was about a foot long and extended about two thirds of the way around my arm. That on my side was about as large as my hand."

A day after the accident, Wilbur was back at work.

Within a month, the Flyer was ready.

Wilbur's wounds were not healing properly, but he was anxious to get into the air. Delagrange and Blériot were captivating the public with their short flights and he was feeling the pressure of their success. Then Farman made a sensational announcement. He was going to America to do some exhibition flying. American promotors had guaranteed him twenty-five thousand dollars!

On August 8 numerous French newspapers appeared with modest headlines: Wilbur Wright May Fly Today.

As usual, Wilbur was up at 7:00 A.M. He brewed coffee, slipped into his overalls, and went out to check the Flyer. He examined it in every possible way. The controls worked. There was gas in the tank. The control wires were taut. The magneto was in good shape. The propeller shafts were sound.

His only problem was that his left arm and side were still sore. He massaged his left fingers. Yes, they were stiff. But, with effort he could control them. The dull pain he could ignore.

By 10:00 A.M. the wooden stands were filled and other spectators were standing around the sides. Many of these people had brought their lunch for they expected numerous delays.

At two o'clock the doors to the "hangar" were opened and the Flyer was pushed out. It was riding on a small cart. As it was being taken toward the catapult, the man who was steadying the right wing relaxed his hold for a moment. And at that moment the bottom of the wing caught on the sharp end of a stump. The cloth was torn. But Wilbur was ready. Taking a needle from his pocket, he made a quick repair by sewing and gluing a patch in place.

Soon the Flyer was up on the catapult ready to fly. Wilbur, however, had disappeared. Moments later, he stepped out of the shed. He had returned to change his clothes! Now, he was dressed in a gray suit complete with collar and tie. But instead of his usual derby, he had donned a cap which he had rakishly put on backwards.

It was 5:00 P.M. before the motor was turned on. Still, Wilbur wasn't ready. He went over the machine again like a doctor with a stethoscope. And it was good that he did, for he found a shorted wire which could have ruined the flight.

Finally Wilbur climbed into his seat. Then he got out in order to question his mechanic about an adjustment. Satisfied that it had been made, he returned to his seat. His wounds were still paining him, but he was ready.

Suddenly the trap was sprung. The Flyer was in the air. A spellbound reporter scribbled: "In a flash the catapult has acted. Mr. Wright has shot into the air, while the spectators gasp in astonishment. At an altitude of thirty feet Wilbur made a sharp turn. Many terrified people felt certain that he was going to crash. Unable to stand the strain, they covered their eyes. Wilbur circled the field twice and then made a perfect landing near the catapult."

"Are you satisfied with your flight?" asked a wide-eyed reporter.

"No. I made at least ten mistakes," replied Wilbur modestly.

The next morning Wilbur's success was in headlines on page 1 all over the United States. But he wasn't finished! That morning he flew again, this time before a crowd of two thousand. Having made an extremely sharp turn before landing, he, and the machine, would have been crushed by the enthusiastic crowd had not a line of policemen kept them away.

Wilbur wanted to fly again, but he was a little unhappy about the sound of the motor. Later in the afternoon, after some more tinkering, Wilbur again climbed into the pilot's seat. This time he had planned a maneuver that would astonish everyone. Instead of circling the field a few times, he made a wide figure eight—the first time this had ever been done in Europe.

The maneuver proved that Wilbur had perfect control. The excitement caused the crowd, even the air-craft experimenters, to lose control. Wilbur explained all of this in a letter to Orville dated August 15.

In the second flight I made an 'eight' and landed at the starting point. The newspapers and the French aviators nearly went wild with excitement. Blériot &

Delagrange were so excited they could barely speak, and Kapferer could only gasp and not talk at all.''

Wilbur continued to make flights, and each time his fame leaped upward. The crowds continued to follow him around, everyone wanted to meet him, to shake his hand, to tell him they admired his persistence. Wilbur soon tired of all of this attention.

After a huge banquet in Paris, he was chided a little because of the brevity of his speech. Wilbur's reply made more headlines. Said this BK, ''I know of only one bird that talks, the parrot, and it can't fly very high.''

On August 19, Orville set out for Washington D.C. The big question in his mind was: Will I succeed in my tests as Wilbur succeeded at Le Mans? Deep inside he was confident that he would. On August 23 he wrote to Wilbur. ''I arrived here Thursday evening, and found that our materials had just arrived and were being hauled to Fort Meyer (a few miles north of the Capitol). . . . The starting point at Fort Meyer is 240 ft. above sea level. . . . I expect to begin the first flight about the first of September.''

Orville was three days late before his first takeoff. But he kept them up—often before wildly cheering crowds. The fact that Glenn Curtiss was among the spectators inspired him to try even harder. Here's the record:

September 4: Four minutes and 15 seconds in the air.
September 7: Fifty-seven seconds in the air.
September 8: Eleven minutes and ten seconds above ground.
September 9: First flight: Fifty-seven minutes and thirty-one seconds above ground. Second flight: One hour and two minutes of circling.

Moreover, Orville continued to fly. On one flight he had a passenger, Lieutenant Frank P. Lahm, and kept him aloft for six minutes and twenty-four seconds. For a public flight, this was a world record. Three days later, he broke this record by flying with Major George O. Squire for nine minutes and six seconds.

Suddenly an ignoring public went wild with acclaim for the two modest BKs. President William Howard Taft invited them and their sister to the White House. The *New York Times* reported: "Miss Wright blushed as she shook the President's hand, but her eyes were alight with pleasure."

Both Wilbur and Orville were presented with gold medals.

This was just the beginning.

Congress voted gold medals and so did the state of Ohio and the city of Dayton. Then Dayton came up with a new idea: fireworks. On the second night of their celebration they lit up the sky with eighty-foot portraits of Wilbur and Orville intertwined with an American flag.

The brothers enjoyed each event. Yet they had work to do. In between receptions and parades, they went into their bicycle shop and worked on the machine they would use in the army tests which had been postponed until July.

With Orville acting as pilot, the tests were duly passed at an average speed of forty-two miles an hour. Since this speed was faster than the one specified by the contract, they received a bonus. That year the United States acquired its first flying machine. It cost thirty thousand dollars.

The slender Bible-believing Bishop's Kids had presented the world with wings.

EPILOGUE

The Wright brothers were now rich. But their natural humility remained. Each was aware of the great influence of his parents. This fact is illustrated by a paragraph in Wilbur's will, written just before his death on May 30, 1912, at the age of 45.

> I hereby give to my father Milton Wright of Dayton, Ohio, my earnest thanks for his example of a courageous, upright life, and for his earnest sympathy with everything tending to my true welfare.

Their home on Hawthorn Street had been one of the cherished centers of their lives, and so when they built their mansion, it was named Hawthorn Hill. Unfortunately, even though Wilbur had worked on the design, he died before it was completed. It was in this Dayton home that Bishop Wright, Orville, and Kate lived.

As for Carrie? She had married Charlie Grumbach, an old friend whom she had known for several years. Nonetheless, she became one of the workers in the new home. The brothers had given her lessons in how to make gravy, and lump-free gravy had become one of her specialties. The Wrights could not get along without her!

None of the Wrights ever lost the common touch. While Wilbur was flying in France in 1909, many celebrities—kings, ambassadors, presidents—asked to fly with him, and he circled around with them. Then one afternoon Wilbur motioned to a shy little boy who had been standing around for a long time. "Let's go for a ride," he said.

After Wilbur landed, his European manager had a question. "Why did you take him up when so many important people are waiting for their chance?" he asked.

"I took up _____ and _____ because *they* wanted me to take them up. I took this boy up because *I* wanted to take him up."

Bishop Milton Wright enjoyed his retirement at Hawthorn Hill. He remained popular. But he never learned how to laugh out loud. Instead, he continued to rumble—often from head to toe. He never tired of relating the positive effect the Bible had had on his children. He died in 1917 at the age of 88.

Katherine Wright—Kate, to Wilbur and Orville—remained at Hawthorn Hill until 1926 when she married Henry J. Haskell, editor and publisher of the *Kansas City Star*. At the time she was 52.

Orville continued to experiment until his death at the age of 76, on January 30, 1948.

Both Orville and Wilbur were men of dreams. But neither was able to envision how far flight would develop. Their biplane with its warping devices gave way to the monoplane and movable ailerons on the edge of each wing. Propellers were given up for jet propulsion.

Speeds of forty miles an hour have now increased to seventeen thousand miles an hour. These speeds have reduced planet earth to a mere village.

In 1969 I was almost breathless as I watched Neil Armstrong descend a ladder and step on the moon. At that moment a little drama was being enacted that I did not know until June 3, 1983. On that date, while gathering material for this book, I was visiting in the

Dayton home of Ivonette Wright Miller, daughter of
Lorin Wright, and thus a niece to Orville and Wilbur.
As I was viewing and photographing various treasures,
Ivonette pointed to a boot.

"Neil Armstrong was wearing that when he stepped
on the moon," she said. "And please look at the top
part."

In the top part there was a tiny section framing a
bit of cloth.

"What is that?" I asked.

"That is a section of the flying-machine which
Wilbur and Orville flew at Kitty Hawk on December
17, 1903!"

From a flight of 852 feet to landing on the moon
in sixty-six years seems incredible. How was it
accomplished? The answer is simple. These
"miracles" were accomplished by following the laws
of God!

Wright Chronology

1828   November 17, Bishop Milton Wright born in a log cabin in Rush County, Indiana.

1831   April 30, Susan Catherine Koerner born at Hillsboro, Virginia.

1846   Bishop Milton Wright converted.

1859   Bishop Wright and Susan Koerner are married.

1861   March 17, first child Reuchlin (Roosh) born.

1862   November 18, Lorin born.

1867   April 16, Wilbur born on a farm near Millville, Indiana.

1868   September, Wright family moves to Hartsville, Indiana.

1869   Wright family moves to Dayton, Ohio.

1871   August 19, Orville Wright born in family home, 7 Hawthorn Street, Dayton, Ohio.

1874   August 19, Katharine born in Hawthorn house.

1878   Bishop Wright returns to Cedar Rapids, Iowa, from a trip, and presents toy helicopter to his children.

1881   Wright family moves to Richmond, Indiana, where Bishop Wright becomes editor of the *Richmond Star.*

1883   Inspired by Barnum's circus, Orville Wright and his friends organize a circus of their own.

1884   Wright family moves back to Dayton, Ohio.

1889   Orville Wright begins to publish the *West Side News*. Later, with Wilbur's help, this becomes *The Evening Item*.

1892   Wilbur and Orville open a bicycle shop at 1005 West Third Street, Dayton. Later, they move to 1034 West Third Street.

1895   Orville invents a calculating machine.

1896   Orville and Wilbur begin to manufacture their own bicycles. Orville is extremely ill with typhoid. In August, Otto Lilienthal, the German glider enthusiast is killed during a glide.

1899   May 30, Wilbur writes to the Smithsonian. July 10, Wilbur gets the idea on how to warp wings. Weeks later, Wilbur flies and warps a five-foot kite. November 27, the Wrights first write to the U.S. Weather Bureau.

1900   May 13, Wilbur writes to Octave Chanute, an aeronautical pioneer. September 6, Wilbur leaves home for Kitty Hawk. September 28, Orville joins him. October, the Wrights test their glider. They make several glides. Glider is wrecked. But they rebuild it with spare parts they had brought along. They leave for Dayton on October 23.

1901   July 27, Wrights reassemble their new glider at Kitty Hawk. They fly it during August and then leave for Dayton on the 20th. Octave Chanute and others witness their flights.

1901   September 18, Wilbur makes a major address to the Western Society of Engineers in Chicago.

1901   October 6, Wilbur and Orville study airlift

with plates on a cycle wheel placed horizontally on another bicycle.

1901 October—December, the Wrights develop their air-tunnel.

1902 August 25, Wrights leave for Kitty Hawk with an enlarged and newly-designed glider. On October 31, they return to Dayton.

1902 Along with their mechanic, Charles Taylor, the Wrights design and build a motor for their new glider—dubbed *the Flyer*.

1903 December 17, 10:35 A.M., Orville achieves world's first powered flight.

1904 September 20, Wilbur achieves first circle flight in a powered aircraft. Eyewitness, Amos I. Root, publishes an account of this feat in *Gleanings in Bee Culture*.

1908 June 20, Wrights inform Glenn Curtiss that the ailerons used on the *June Bug* infringe their patents.

1909 February 3, Wilbur demonstrates their latest aircraft in France.

1909 May 13, the Wrights are given great welcome in Dayton.

1912 May 30, Wilbur dies of typhoid fever in Dayton.

1948 January 30, Orville dies of a heart attack in Dayton.

BIBLIOGRAPHY

American Heritage. Editors. *History of Flight* (American Heritage, 1962).

Combs, Harry. *Kill Devil Hill* (Houghton Mifflin, 1979).

Crouch, Tom D. *A Dream of Wings* (W. W. Norton, 1981).

Freudenthal, Elizabeth E. *Flight into History* (University of Oklahoma, 1949).

Gibbs—Smith, Charles H. *Flight through the Ages* (T. Y. Crowell, 1974).

Gibbs—Smith, Charles H. *The Invention of the Aeroplane* (Taplinger Publishing Co., 1966).

Goldstrom, John. *Narrative History of Aviation* (Macmillan, 1930).

Hallion, Richard P. *The Wright Brothers, Heirs of Prometheus* (The Smithsonian Institution, 1978).

Kelly, Fred C. *Miracle at Kitty Hawk* (Arno Press, 1972).

Kelly, Fred C. *The Wright Brothers* (Ballantine Books, 1956).

McFarland, Marvin W. *The Papers of Wilbur and Orville Wright* Vol. I and II (McGraw Hill, 1953).

McMahon, John R. *The Wright Brothers, Fathers of Flight* (Little Brown, 1930).

Milbank, Jeremiah, Jr., *The First Century of Flight in America* (Princeton University Press, 1943).

Miller, Ivonette Wright. *Wright Reminiscences* (Ivonette Wright Miller, 1978).

Nolan, Patrick B. and Zamonski, John A. *The Wright Brothers Collection* (Garland Publishing, Inc., 1977).

Walsh, John Evangelist. *One Day at Kitty Hawk* (T. Y. Crowell, 1975).

Wheelman. November 1980 issue (The Wheelman Magazine, 1980).

INDEX

SOWERS SERIES

ATHLETE
Billy Sunday, Home Run to Heaven
by Robert Allen

EXPLORERS AND PIONEERS
Christopher Columbus, Adventurer of Faith and Courage
by Bennie Rhodes
Johnny Appleseed, God's Faithful Planter, John Chapman
by David Collins

HOMEMAKERS
Abigail Adams, First Lady of Faith and Courage
by Evelyn Witter
Susanna Wesley, Mother of John and Charles
by Charles Ludwig

HUMANITARIANS
Jane Addams, Founder of Hull House
by David Collins
Florence Nightingale, God's Servant at the Battlefield
by David Collins
Teresa of Calcutta, Serving the Poorest of the Poor
by D. Jeanene Watson
Clara Barton, God's Soldier of Mercy
by David Collins

MUSICIANS AND POETS
Francis Scott Key, God's Courageous Composer
by David Collins
Samuel Francis Smith, My Country, 'Tis of Thee
by Marguerite E. Fitch